David Pinski

TREASURE

in a new adaption by Colin Chambers
from a translation by Ludwig Lewisohn

OBERON BOOKS
LONDON

WWW.OBERONBOOKS.COM

First published in 2015 by Oberon Books Ltd
521 Caledonian Road, London N7 9RH
Tel: +44 (0) 20 7607 3637 / Fax: +44 (0) 20 7607 3629
e-mail: info@oberonbooks.com
www.oberonbooks.com

Der Oytzer © David Pinski, 1910

David Pinski is hereby identified as author of this play
in accordance with section 77 of the Copyright, Designs and
Patents Act 1988.

English adaptation *Treasure* © Colin Chambers, 2015

Colin Chambers is hereby identified adaptor of this play
in accordance with section 77 of the Copyright, Designs and
Patents Act 1988. The author has asserted his moral rights.

All rights whatsoever in this play are strictly reserved
and application for performance etc. should be made
before commencement of rehearsal to Macnaughton Lord
Representation, 44 South Molton Street, London W1K 5RT
(info@mlrep.com). No performance may be given unless a licence
has been obtained, and no alterations may be made in the title or
the text of the play without the author's prior written consent.

You may not copy, store, distribute, transmit, reproduce or
otherwise make available this publication (or any part of it) in
any form, or binding or by any means (print, electronic, digital,
optical, mechanical, photocopying, recording or otherwise),
without the prior written permission of the publisher. Any person
who does any unauthorized act in relation to this publication may
be liable to criminal prosecution and civil claims for damages.

A catalogue record for this book is available from the British
Library.

PB ISBN: 9781783199990
E ISBN: 9781783192625

Cover design © Leo Baeck Institute

Visit www.oberonbooks.com to read more about all our books
and to buy them. You will also find features, author interviews and
news of any author events, and you can sign up for e-newsletters
so that you're always first to hear about our new releases.

To my granddaughter Everly

Introduction

David Pinski, the author of *Treasure*, was born in 1872 in Mogilev, then part of the Russian Empire, now a city in eastern Belarus. In his youth, he moved several times, from Vitebsk and Moscow to Vienna, Warsaw, Berlin and Basel, before heading in 1899 for New York at the invitation of the editor of a newspaper to which he had been contributing. He lived there for the next fifty years until he emigrated to the newly born state of Israel where he died, in Haifa, in 1959.

A Socialist and a Zionist, Pinski spoke several languages and was a prolific writer, of essays, poems, novels and plays. He made most impact through his Yiddish writing, becoming one of the leading playwrights in that language. He was active in Jewish cultural and political life, particularly through his extensive work on a variety of publications, and as President of the Jewish National Workers' Alliance, President of the Jewish Cultural Society, and the first President of the Yiddish PEN Club.

Yiddish theatre proliferated at the end of the nineteenth century across eastern and central Europe as well as in areas of significant Jewish settlement in America and Britain and elsewhere. In New York, Pinski became a prominent and founding member of the Yiddish Theatre Society and its journal *Tealit*. He was known in his plays for his sympathetic treatment of workers – in *Isaac Sheftel* (1899), for example, which tells the story of an exploited weaver – and for his at the time daring handling of desire, as seen in the depiction of sexual appetite in *Yankel the Blacksmith* (1906), which was turned into a film in the 1930s. He also wrote about figures from legend and folk myth, often drawn from the Bible, and in *The Family Tsvi* (1904) he confronted the need for Jewish resistance.

Of Pinski's more than sixty plays, a couple have earned a minor place in theatrical history. The first play performed by the Hebrew-language theatre Habimah in Moscow under Stanislavsky's patronage was Pinski's *Der Eybiger Yid* ('The Eternal Jew') in 1919, and the Federal Theatre Project staged his play *The Tailor Becomes a Storekeeper* in Yiddish in Chicago and

New York in 1938, leading to it become the only new Yiddish play of the Project's to be cited at the hearings of the House Committee to Investigate Un-American Activities where it was denounced as 'pro-union propaganda'.

Probably Pinski's most successful play is *Der Oytzer*, completed in 1906, which is adapted in this text as *Treasure*. It was first performed in Berlin in German in 1911, directed by Max Reinhardt, but remained popular in the Yiddish repertoire from its debut in New York in 1912 through to the 1940s. Pinski himself appeared in one production. An English-language version was seen at the Garrick Theatre on Broadway in 1920, staged by the Theatre Guild and starring Celia Adler, and there was also a production in the Vilna Ghetto in 1943. The play, portions of which were often improvised, appeared in places as far apart as Warsaw and Buenos Aires, and for several productions Pinski revised his text.

I came across the play some years ago after I left the Royal Shakespeare Company, where I had been Literary Manager, when two American friends and I decided to explore Yiddish theatre, a wonderfully vibrant popular theatre that was in danger of being – or already had been – forgotten. We wanted to see whether any of the plays could satisfy a contemporary audience and transcend the moment and conditions of their creation. I read Pinski's play in a 1915 English translation by Ludwig Lewisohn and thought it fitted the bill. I adapted it for the present without, I hope, losing its roots in the past. The main changes I made were to cut the dialogue, which in the original is often repetitious, and to set the action in two acts rather than four. In order to meet the casting needs of the Finborough production, further, slight, amendments were made, such as conflating a few small roles and giving names to generic townspeople. This production, I believe, is the British premiere of the play and offers an opportunity to see the extent to which *Treasure* can cross time and cultures and still speak to us today.

Colin Chambers
Autumn 2015

With thanks and acknowledgements to Gabriel Pinski
and the rest of the Pinski estate

Characters

Jachne-Braine, married to Chone

Tille, their daughter

Judke, their son

Chone, the Gravedigger

Marriage Broker

Soskin, Chief Citizen and Capitalist

President of the Congregation

Reb Itsche, from the Society for Providing Poor Maidens with a Dowry

Rifkele, from the Society for Providing Poor Maidens with a Dowry

Reb Chaim, from the Society for the Care of the Sick

Manke, from the Society for the Care of the Sick

Reb Joseph, from the Fraternal Burial Society

Reb Faivish, from the Fraternal Burial Society

Merkin, a Lawyer

Sarah, a pregnant woman

Aaron, her husband

Morevskaya, a Teacher

Jacob, from the town

Yekel, from the town

Newcomer

Boy 1

Boy 2

Boy 3

Yankev, from the town

Hersh, from the town

Hindel, from the town

Well-Dressed Man

Holy Rabbi

Townspeople

The Dead

The Russian pale, early 1900s. High summer. The action takes place in the home of the town's gravedigger and in the local cemetery on the fast day that commemorates the destruction of Jerusalem, and on the following day.

ACT ONE

SCENE 1

An untidy white-washed room. A few chairs. Two windows give on to a cemetery. The right-hand one is open. Between the windows, a dilapidated leather sofa, in front of which stands a folding table. Bedding is strewn over the sofa. To the left, a door that leads to the kitchen and outer hall. The stove protrudes to the left of this door. Beside it there is a bench. To the right of the door is an old, glass-fronted cupboard with drawers. Downstage right is an unmade bed. Above the bed hangs a bundle of clothes wrapped in a sheet. Next to the bed is a second door, which leads to another room.

JACHNE-BRAINE sits on a footstool downstage centre. Her toes stick out through her stockings. She wears an old red cloth tied round her head.

TILLE sits by the right-hand window. She wears an old frayed green corset. She has carefully combed her hair and gathered it in a bun, with curls falling over her forehead. She leans back in her chair and admires herself in the small mirror that stands on the window sill. She arranges her curls again.

JACHNE-BRAINE: *(Slowly reading aloud from a song of lamentation.)* The Israelites who used…on the Passover… to eat of the sacrifice of the Passover…they have eaten for hunger…the heads of asses and satisfied their hunger… with bitterness. Our sins are wound about our necks… and God hath said: I will remember your sins….and ye shall eat of the flesh of your children. And because your daughters…

Voices off. Above them a high-pitched wail.

Oh. There's the funeral. And you're looking in a mirror. It's a widow, not a widower.

She continues reading.

And because the daughters of Jerusalem have boasted of their beauty and have said, when…the Babylonians

13

come…they will make us to be their wives and…therefore it came to pass that when…the Babylonians came to Jerusalem and…took them unto themselves, God smote them with a leprosy and when…the Babylonians saw this, they…cast forth the women and the wheel of the chariot passed over their head and…

(To TILLE.) Better you listen than look at yourself in the mirror.

(Reads.) And because the daughters of Jerusalem boasted of their beauty…

(To TILLE.) You don't comb your hair for days on end. But today, a day of fast, because it is forbidden, you go and build a tower on your head.

(Reads.) …and they will make us to be their wives…

(To TILLE.) Get away from the window, I'm telling you. Away. There'll be no Babylonian passing by and no man will come to the graves today to look for a wife.

TILLE: Don't let me get in your way. You carry on with your lamentations.

JACHNE-BRAINE: Imagine. There she sits, displaying herself, staring at the mirror. *(Reads.)* …and took them unto themselves, God smote them with a leprosy…

Breaks off.

Just look how she sits. Get away from that window, I say. Leprosy is what you deserve. Oh, God almighty!

Wailing of many women. A funeral procession passes the windows with its coffin. The cries of one woman stand out: 'Who will care for me now? My seven children. Take me as well, almighty Father.'

TILLE: How terrible.

JACHNE-BRAINE: And you stare at the mirror.

TILLE: What will she do? The poor woman. Seven children. She'll starve. Who'd marry a woman with seven kids?

JACHNE-BRAINE: Specially when the virgins sit by the window and pop their eyes out of their heads.

TILLE: Oh do shut up. Did you find that in your book?

JACHNE-BRAINE: In my book it is written that you are to put away that mirror and get away from that window.

TILLE: Why does it upset you so much? You grudge me even that?

JACHNE-BRAINE: Better you sit here and read with me.

TILLE: I never go out to town. I can't show myself. I've got nothing to put on. At least let me sit here and see a few human beings. When can I do it if not today? It has to be a funeral or a fast day if there're to be people about.

JACHNE-BRAINE: What use in talking? Waste my breath! When people come, she acts like she's in a shop window.

TILLE: And why shouldn't I? *(Laughs.)* Come here and see for yourself. There goes a handsome young man. It's a real pleasure just looking at him. Look. Look now. *(She looks in the mirror.)* From the moment he catches sight of me, he can't take his eyes off me, and then he comes closer and closer…

JACHNE-BRAINE: *(Jumps up.)* This minute. Now. Away from the window.

TILLE: He isn't looking. He isn't looking at all. You have no imagination.

JACHNE-BRAINE: *(Sits.)* What a girl. Oh, what a girl.

TILLE: You don't understand what it is to dream.

JACHNE-BRAINE: Oh, of course not. Just listen to her. I don't know what it is to dream! I wish all my bad dreams would escape from my head and enter yours…

TILLE: I mean conscious dreams. To be awake and to dream…to sit here and dream.

JACHNE-BRAINE: A great happiness that must be to you, I'm sure. Leave me be to get on with my reading. And get away from the window. It's not your business to sit there and dream. *(Scornfully.)* Dream!

(Reads again.) And when they saw this they cast them forth...

TILLE: It's beautiful to dream. Like a lovely story. You forget yourself. Wafted far away...you become something different... I sit here and think and think and I am suddenly none other than Lady Rothschild.

JACHNE-BRAINE: No more, no less?

TILLE: The Rothschild bride. Why not? He's rich, doesn't need a dowry. I see him filling great sacks of gold and setting off out into the world to seek a wife. He travels and travels until he lands in our town. He comes to the cemetery and finds me sitting by the window.

JACHNE-BRAINE: Do stop your talking. It makes me feel sick. You should be locked up in a madhouse.

TILLE: He falls to his knees before me and proclaims: I love you. I am Rothschild. Will you marry me?

JACHNE-BRAINE: Will you stop? I'll throw something.

TILLE: *(Laughs.)* Sometimes I dream that a Count is coming...

JACHNE-BRAINE: What? A Christian? Whatever next!

TILLE: I only dream it. You can imagine anything.

JACHNE-BRAINE: Fine dreams, fine! Like those in my book. The daughters of Jerusalem boast of their beauty and say when the Babylonians come they will make us their wives... May death fall upon you. On a fast day she has nothing better to do than dream the devil knows what.

TILLE: What's the harm? Marriage is a matter for us Jews and so is money. And I dream of marriage and I dream of money. When I think of all that money...

JACHNE-BRAINE: Stop talking. I tell you, stop talking and let me read.

TILLE: Let me go on. I'll tell you what I'd do if I had all that money. I would rule the world. I can feel myself becoming...

JACHNE-BRAINE: Damn you!

(Angry, she reads again.) And He hath made heavier my sorrow and hath made a mockery of me before all the heathen...

> *JUDKE enters from outside. He has a patchy, thin beard and long, unkempt hair under a torn cap. He wears rags. He has a withered arm and leg. Saliva runs down his chin.*

JUDKE: *(Sobbing.)* Uh, uh, uh, uh.

TILLE: Judke. What's the matter?

JACHNE-BRAINE: *(Irritably.)* Why are you crying? Are you hurt?

JUDKE: Uh, uh, uh, uh... Buried dog... I buried...

JACHNE-BRAINE: Oh, what fine grounds for grief. What a lamentation. *(Mocking him.)* Uh, uh, uh, uh.

> *TILLE laughs.*

JUDKE: *(Angrily to TILLE.)* Schutschke dead! Schutschke buried! No laugh...*(Stands by the bench, facing away towards the stove.)* I love him... *(Unconsciously imitates the voice of the wailing widow.)* Why have you deserted me? *(Throws himself face down on the bench and howls. TILLE laughs but stops herself at once and puts her hand over her mouth. JUDKE goes to her, face distorted with rage.)* You stop laughing or I kill you... I...stop your mouth... I throttle you. *(He grinds his teeth and extends the clenched fist of his stronger arm toward her.)*

TILLE: *(Jumps up to soothe him.)* No, no Judke. I'm not laughing. I didn't mean to laugh. It just...came out, on its own. Don't be angry and don't cry. Don't cry, you poor thing.

JUDKE: You always laugh. I see it in your eyes.

TILLE: I am not laughing. It is my eyes, not me. I am serious. It's a real shame.

JUDKE: I loved him so…

TILLE: He was a very good dog.

JUDKE: Could do anything. Stand on hind legs. Offer paw. *(Sobs.)* Uh…uh, uh.

JACHNE-BRAINE: Stop howling. Stop. Just listen to that howling.

JUDKE: *(Angrily.)* Your fault Schutschke dead. You broke his leg.

JACHNE-BRAINE: If only I'd broken yours too.

JUDKE: You wait. I found money, give you nothing. I dug grave for Schutschke and found gold coins. *(He takes something from his pocket.)* See? But I…

JACHNE-BRAINE: *(Cries out.)* What did you find?

TILLE: *(Looks in his hand.)* They really are gold coins. I'm sure they're sovereigns.

JACHNE-BRAINE: Sovereigns? Sovereigns? Lots?

JUDKE: *(Grinning. To JACHNE-BRAINE.)* You see? *(He puts the money back in his pocket.)*

JACHNE-BRAINE: Where did you find them? How many?

JUDKE: Hah, hah, hah.

JACHNE-BRAINE: *(To TILLE.)* Many? Has he many?

TILLE: Quite a lot. Definitely more than ten. *(To JUDKE.)* Show them. Let's count them.

JUDKE: No! Won't! She shan't see!

JACHNE-BRAINE: This very minute you are to show me what you have found. *(To TILLE.)* How much is a sovereign? Much money?

TILLE: How should I know? A great deal, I think. Fifteen roubles at least.

JACHNE-BRAINE: Oh my God. Fifteen roubles! How many did you say he had? More than ten?

TILLE: Certainly. Perhaps many more. A whole pile. Two hundred roubles maybe.

JACHNE-BRAINE: *(To JUDKE.)* This very minute you hand over what you have found. Do you hear what your mother is saying or not? This minute. Now. Hand it over. Two hundred roubles! Oh my God. If you don't give it to me this very minute of your own free will I will take a stick and I will leave not a single limb on your whole body.

JUDKE: *(Cries as if possessed.)* No! No! No! Won't!

TILLE: *(Whispers to JACHNE-BRAINE.)* Let him be. He'll hand it over later of his own accord.

JACHNE-BRAINE: Oh my God. Two hundred roubles! Did you ever hear of letting a crazy person keep two hundred roubles. I'm getting dressed and going to the police.

JUDKE: *(Beside himself.)* I'll throttle you! Throttle you!

TILLE: Leave him. Why must you always provoke him? Do you want his attacks to start again? *(To JUDKE.)* Don't be frightened, Judke. She won't go to the police.

JACHNE-BRAINE: Who knows? Perhaps he stole the money!

TILLE: Why do you always talk that way? You know he didn't steal it.

JUDKE: Didn't steal! Stole yourself! I don't steal. *(To TILLE, as he quickly takes his hand from his pocket and presses the money into her hand.)* There. All of it. Give it to you! Give her nothing. You hear? Nothing. I throttle her. Stole herself.

He falls by the bench in a convulsion. TILLE, surprised at having her hands full of money, puts the coins in her pocket and hurries to JUDKE. She opens his shirt, goes to the kitchen and returns with a cup of water.

JACHNE-BRAINE: *(Searches his pockets and opens his hands while TILLE is out.)* Nothing left. *(She tries to reach into TILLE's pocket.)*

TILLE: *(Busy with JUDKE, thrusts her mother's hand away with her elbow.)* Leave it. Wait. There's plenty of time.

JACHNE-BRAINE: Just give me the money.

TILLE: Patience. We will think this over. We must discuss this a bit more.

JACHNE-BRAINE: Are you crazy? What's wrong with you? Think it over indeed! What's there to discuss? This very minute you are to give me the money.

TILLE: I will if I want to, if it suits me. But I don't even have the right to. You heard for yourself. He forbad me to give any money to you.

JACHNE-BRAINE: Are you serious?

TILLE: Quite serious. Since the money was given to me it belongs to me. And what he forbad I must not do. But because I'm a good girl... Come on, hold out your hand and I'll count. *(She places coins into JACHNE-BRAINE's hand.)* One, two, three... Do you see? Gold sovereigns. Now you're like the wife of a wealthy factory owner. But not a word. Say nothing to him. Wait! Here's another. Four. Now you're really rich. And just to keep you quiet, here is one more. Five! Now say thank you.

JACHNE-BRAINE: Is that all?

TILLE: Yes. You won't get any more.

JACHNE-BRAINE: And now I'll take that stick and I'll...oh, five coins is all she gives me.

TILLE: You don't want them? Give them back, then.

JACHNE-BRAINE: I'll give you what for. You'll wonder where you came from. Hand over the money. All of it!

TILLE: People are never satisfied, whatever you do.

JACHNE-BRAINE: All of the money you are going to give to me. Or else just you watch out…

CHONE enters in a hurry. He wears his ritual garment over his shirt and trousers, fixed with a belt.

CHONE: What's all this noise? It can be heard outside! What money? What's the matter? He's lying there and she's…

JACHNE-BRAINE: Tell her to give me the money at once. Two hundred roubles. Oh my God.

TILLE closes the window.

CHONE: Money? Two hundred roubles? What gibberish are you talking?

JACHNE-BRAINE: Tell her to hand it over. Judke found it. What right has she got to take it?

TILLE: That's not the way it is. I've taken nothing. He gave it to me himself.

CHONE: *(Spits.)* I can't make head nor tail of your chatter. Explain in words of one syllable.

JACHNE-BRAINE: Listen to him. Suddenly he's left his brains at the door. What is it you don't understand? What?… Judke buried the dog and found gold sovereigns. Clear enough? Understood now? And now will you tell her to hand over the money. What right has she to take it? Have you found your brains at last? Why do you stand there like a block of wood? *(To TILLE.)* Hand over the money. Do you hear?

CHONE: Just wait a second and let me think. Judke has buried the dog and he found gold sovereigns… Where did he bury him? Where did he find the coins?

JACHNE-BRAINE: As if I know? Could I even speak to him?

CHONE: *(To TILLE.)* Where? Where did he find them?

JACHNE-BRAINE: *(Mockingly.)* Where? Where did he find them? Why does that interest you? He made a find. That's it. That's enough. Now see to it…

CHONE: You're so clever, oh wise one. Perhaps, in that place, there is…

TILLE: Yes! Of course! *(She runs to JUDKE.)*

JACHNE-BRAINE: What does that mean: 'Perhaps, in that place…'

CHONE: *(Looks about to check they are alone and whispers.)* Perhaps, in that place, there is – treasure?

JACHNE-BRAINE: Ah, ah. *(Drops onto a chair.)* Ah, I feel sick. My legs are going under me. It's true.

TILLE: Judke, Judke! Can't you hear? He hasn't come round yet.

CHONE: How is it it didn't occur to you to ask at the very first! May you burn in… Ay, quarrel. That's what you can do. I'll beat you to death. I'll tear you limb from limb. And today – the cemetery is crawling with people.

TILLE: He is sure to have filled the hole. So why do you curse like that?

CHONE: She wants to be in the right also. Why do I curse? What? Hand over the money this second. Give it here now. *(To JACHNE-BRAINE.)* How much did he find? How much?

JACHNE-BRAINE: Did I count it? Here are five.

TILLE: And those I gave to her.

JACHNE-BRAINE: Do you hear those words? Behold our benefactress. A whole pile she still has on her. More than ten pieces for certain.

CHONE: *(Grasps the five coins like a hungry man and stares at them.)* Sovereigns. Sovereigns. Treasure. Definitely treasure for sure. Oh, that I could bury you all on one and the same day. *(To TILLE.)* Hand it over. Give me the money NOW.

TILLE: You really mean that? You're joking.

CHONE: You will give me all the money you have in your pocket. *(With clenched teeth.)* Out with it.

TILLE: Do I look like a fool? *(CHONE rushes towards her but she steps out of the way and uses the table as a barrier.)* I am to give you all the money and then starve until you drop me a kopek. I'll have to come begging for the slightest thing. Judke made me a present of the money and so it is mine. I won't have it taken from me. It is my dowry. Or maybe you have provided me with one perhaps? I don't want to stay single until I'm old and grey. I must have a dowry. Give me my dowry. Give me my dowry.

CHONE: Yes…but why did you take it all? We have need of it too.

TILLE: I did not take it all. You have a share.

CHONE: Five sovereigns?

TILLE: It's enough. You'll soon be rid of me. If you need more, you'll always be able to get it at my house. More easily than I can in yours. I really don't understand why you want to take all the money from me. What right do you have? What do I want to do with it? Provide for myself. I just want to buy myself an ever so modest husband.

CHONE: *(To JACHNE-BRAINE.)* What do you say to your daughter, eh?

JACHNE-BRAINE: May she break…oh my God, oh my God.

CHONE: I only want to avoid…

TILLE: Come on. Don't bother. You know nothing escapes the grave.

JUDKE suddenly gets up.

You'd better ask him.

CHONE: *(To TILLE.)* You won't escape me. Hey, Judke. *(JUDKE goes to the door.)* Where did you find the coins? *(JUDKE continues walking.)* Come here, I say. Where did you bury Schutschke?

JUDKE: *(At the door.)* Won't tell.

CHONE: Why not? I order you.

JUDKE: Won't.

CHONE: Where was it? In the cemetery? Behind the wall? In the old field? Or in the new one?

JUDKE: *(Grinning.)* Ha...ha...ha...

CHONE: *(Taking off his belt.)* You will tell me at once. Or – you see this? I'll beat you black and blue.

JUDKE: *(Clenches his fist and hisses.)* Won't tell.

He runs out.

TILLE: *(About to follow him.)* He'll tell me. I'll run after him.

CHONE: Aha! You want to sneak away, do you?

TILLE: I don't have to sneak off. But we ought to know where the hole is and see what's there. Imagine if there really is treasure there.

CHONE: First I want the money you have.

TILLE: You're off again. And all the while Judke is getting further away and we won't be able to find him. *(She goes towards the door.)*

CHONE: *(Blocking her path.)* You will not leave this room until you have given me all the money.

TILLE: But he may even begin to dig again and someone may see him.

CHONE: The coins!

TILLE: I am only thinking of you. I have this money...

JACHNE-BRAINE: Let her go. He may start to dig and then others will see.

TILLE: There might be a whole treasure and he thinks he only needs the few coins I have here.

JACHNE-BRAINE: You'd better run after Judke. Let her go.

CHONE: First I want the money she is hiding.

TILLE: *(To JACHNE-BRAINE.)* I could easily escape through the window, but if it means nothing to him to lose the treasure then it need mean nothing to me either. Think – treasure. No, really, I can jump from the window. *(She goes to the window.)*

JACHNE-BRAINE: She'll do it.

CHONE rushes towards TILLE. JUDKE returns, crying.

JUDKE: Hu...hu...hu.

The others turn toward him.

JACHNE-BRAINE: *(The first to find words.)* Whatever's wrong with you again? What's happened? Have you been robbed?

JUDKE: I can't find Schutschke's grave.

JACHNE-BRAINE: There you are!

CHONE: What does this mean, you can't find it?

JUDKE: Forgot where I buried him.

JACHNE-BRAINE: Oh my God.

TILLE: You have your treasure now.

CHONE: What? Forgotten?

JACHNE-BRAINE: Liar!

JUDKE: *(Angrily.)* Hay, hay, hay.

TILLE: He doesn't lie. Is it the first time he's forgotten something after one of his attacks?

JACHNE-BRAINE: *(In despair.)* That's what comes of getting involved with crazy Judke.

CHONE: Can't you remember at all? In the cemetery or behind the cemetery?

JUDKE: I buried him deep in the earth. Filled the hole. Put up a little board – gravestone. Cut into it with my knife:

Schutschke, rest in peace. I don't know where anymore.
I…maybe wall…maybe tree…

TILLE: Shall we help you look?

JUDKE: Don't know where. Find no more…

> *Stretches himself out on the bench and whines. Sound of weeping
> and wailing off right.*

TILLE: We must go and look all over the cemetery for the board.

JACHNE-BRAINE: Of all things! You can go and look long
and hard.

TILLE: You don't think it's worth it?

CHONE: Who knows whether they're any coins left or
whether he took them all with him?

TILLE: Who could understand what he said?

CHONE: *(Enraged.)* Oh, no, you couldn't do that! But you
could drive him into convulsions. You could do that.

TILLE: It's not my fault he had an attack.

CHONE: It was you who began it. You. Didn't you just have
to hurry to wrench the coins from him.

TILLE: Same over and over again. I wrenched nothing from
him and didn't… *(Turns to JACHNE-BRAINE.)* Mother…

CHONE: May you all be struck down on one and the same
day. *(To TILLE.)* Mark this. I have no time for you now and
no strength, but I will get the money out of you to the last
kopek. You will count it out to me on this very table or I will
beat you to death.

TILLE: Oh, ho.

CHONE: Be very certain you will hand it all over.
To the very last kopek. I have another burial to attend to
now. Oh, that I could bury you all as well. Don't go running
around the cemetery looking for the coins. There are too
many people about. And, you know-alls, hold your tongues.

He exits.

TILLE: A fat lot he's going to get from me.

She jumps on the bed, takes down a hat and coat wrapped up in the sheet and puts them on. She checks in the mirror.

JACHNE-BRAINE: Where are you off to?

TILLE: To find a safe place for the money and provide for myself.

JACHNE-BRAINE: Where are you going with all that money? To show off all over town? Hand it over!

TILLE: Don't start up again, mother. Not again. Oh, it's a funny sensation, having money in your pocket, I can tell you. Do you know, mother, money warms you. If you knew how warm and safe I feel. Like a new creature in a new skin. Think of it. Tille Chone, the gravedigger's daughter, the eternal beggar, suddenly has money in her pocket. *(She taps her pocket.)* Hear how it jingles. And Judke will remember and we will find the treasure. Oh, mother, all the treasure. Oh, oh, it makes me dizzy. Why, we may become rich beyond imagination. We may become millionaires. I'll turn the world upside down.

JACHNE-BRAINE: Just listen to her trying to confuse me with all that blather.

TILLE: I am ready. Dressed and – elegant. To be sure, my hat is ready for the dunghill, and so is the coat and the frock most of all. But now I have money. Mother, I feel I must give you a kiss.

She runs to her and embraces her.

JACHNE-BRAINE: *(Thrusts her away.)* Get away from me. Go with a kind heart, I say.

She tries to reach TILLE's pocket.

TILLE: Hey. Leave that alone. *(She pushes her hand away.)* That's stealing. That's not allowed. Now then, goodbye. Goodbye Judke. Don't cry, Judke, and remember.

(To JACHNE-BRAINE.) If he goes to the cemetery, follow him. Don't fall asleep over your book. I'll be back later.

She hurries out.

JACHNE-BRAINE: What a creature she is. What a creature. Oh, God help me.

The sound of wailing comes from the cemetery. JACHNE-BRAINE opens the window and the wailing is heard more loudly. She stands there for a moment, then resumes her seat.

Treasure. Treasure. Another burial. Oh, oh, oh.

She sits and begins to read.

SCENE 2

Same room. Same day. Dusk. The table is covered with an old tablecloth and has on it a lamp, samovar, loaf of bread, plates, glasses, spoons and knives. JACHNE-BRAINE sits by the right-hand window, holding her head with one hand. JUDKE sits on the bench.·

JACHNE-BRAINE: Father will be back soon from prayers and she's not here. Where could she have disappeared to? Where? You might go to your aunt and see?

JUDKE: *(Angrily.)* She'll come by herself.

JACHNE-BRAINE: Ah, my heart tells me she'll have spread it everywhere and if people hear, we'll have the whole town arriving before nightfall. Why do you just sit there? Why don't you go and look yourself?

JUDKE: Can't find. Don't know. I forgot. Not my business.

JACHNE-BRAINE: Not his business! Forgotten is what he's done. Heap of wretchedness. Ah, what children. And the other one – a gossiping gad-about-town. Father will show her!

A carriage is heard approaching. The door slams. JACHNE-BRAINE gets up.

Who's coming?

TILLE enters wearing an expensive new dress and a lace hat with tall feathers. She carries a lace-embroidered silk parasol, white gloves, a bandbox and a package. She has rings on two fingers and wears earrings. JACHNE-BRAINE and JUDKE are dumb with astonishment. TILLE bursts out laughing. JACHNE-BRAINE recovers.

Oh, dear, dear me, dear me. Behold. And maybe you even came in a carriage.

TILLE: *(Laughing.)* Who else? In a cab. Now, mother, only the bridegroom is missing. My wedding clothes I have.

Walks up and down pretending to be a fashionable lady.

JUDKE: *(Laughs.)* Ho, ho, ho, hee, hee, hee.

He continues to laugh, explosively from time to time.

TILLE: How do you like me? Do you like the dress? I bought it at Seldowitch's.

JACHNE-BRAINE: At Seldowitch's!

TILLE: Well, what do you think? That I would go to the first shop I came across. This dress was made for Schmerling's daughter. She died this week just before her wedding. I got it for a song. And look at the hat. Straight from Paris.

JACHNE-BRAINE: Oh my God. I don't see how you can have the effrontery to buy such a hat for yourself. God only knows what it cost.

TILLE: Even so. Haven't I got the money? Look how it suits me. Lovely, eh? *(Opens the bandbox.)* And here I have – look and admire – a cloak. Straight from Gershunski.

JACHNE-BRAINE: You are crazy. They didn't show you the door?

TILLE: No one shows you the door if you pay with good money. Look how well the cloak fits. As if made to order. Don't you think so? And I have something else. The parasol. It's silk. Look at the lace – and the gloves – fine kid.

29

JACHNE-BRAINE: Oh my God. Have you spent all the money?

TILLE: Wait. The main item is yet to come.

JACHNE-BRAINE: *(Frightened.)* Yet to come?

TILLE: *(Shaking the earrings and then showing her hand.)* See how it sparkles and gleams? This is diamond number one and this is diamond number two. And now. What time is it? *(She displays a gold watch and chain.)* Well, how do you like it? And – do you think that's all? I have ordered another dress from Seldowitch's.

JACHNE-BRAINE: All the money! All the money!

TILLE: Patience. I have something else. But this is for you. *(She opens the package.)* Look, for a dress, for you. Real wool. Pure wool. Twelve yards. It cost a lot of money. Just look at the kind of stuff it is.

JACHNE-BRAINE: *(Throws the cloth down.)* May you break your neck and burn with all your 'stuff'. Who begged you for it? Who?

TILLE: My kind heart. Because I am a good daughter. How can anyone bear to buy for themselves alone? *(She picks up the cloth and dusts it off.)* All the days of your life you've not worn such cloth and now you throw it on the ground. A crime for certain. Come here, Judke, and look at this. It's for suits for you and father. Fit for a prince.

JUDKE: *(Climbs from the bench and admires the cloth. Giggling, he strokes it.)* Beautiful. Beautiful. Dress myself up fine. We go walking. Arm in arm.

> *Takes her arm and walks up and down with her. He remains standing, giggling, admiring, touching, sniffing her new clothes.*

JACHNE-BRAINE: *(Stunned.)* All the money. What's the sense of that?

TILLE: Sense! Sense! Must everything be sensible?

JACHNE-BRAINE: A fine answer. Oh, it's too much. There's your dowry now. Give me my dowry, she cries. Give me my dowry. And then goes and throws the money away, to the four winds, for nothing, to the devil! And by this time surely the whole town knows.

TILLE: You should have seen. The street was thick with people. From all corners they came running to see the sovereigns.

JACHNE-BRAINE: Oh, I'll kill myself. I'll take whatever comes to hand and split open your skull. The whole town will be here to look for the treasure.

TILLE: Calm down. No one will come. I'm not so stupid as to tell people the treasure is still lying somewhere in the cemetery. No. I did even better. I told them we had all the treasure already. You should have seen them. They all believe we are millionaires.

JACHNE-BRAINE: A great happiness, for you I'm sure but have you considered what your nonsense may end in?

TILLE: Suppose I have? What then? If I have considered it twenty times over, what of it?

JACHNE-BRAINE: What of it? People will demand of millionaires that they behave like millionaires.

TILLE: I have the best answers to that question. Quite a number in fact. In the first place, there are money millionaires. Well, we're that kind. In the second place...

JACHNE-BRAINE: Oh my God. A fine mess she has made for us. Your father will lose his position. The town won't let a millionaire be their gravedigger. Because of you we'll all have to go begging yet.

TILLE: Oh, don't let's have any more wailing. Why should it cost him his job? Is he depriving anyone else of it? Is he asking for more wages? And if he's a miserly millionaire, who's harmed by that? And, in the second place – do try to understand – in the second place we will meanwhile hunt for the treasure. Judke will probably remember anyhow.

JUDKE: Can't at all.

JACHNE-BRAINE: Exactly. And what happens if you search and find and there's nothing there except the body of a dog, if there's nothing but the coins Judke already found and which are now gone too?

TILLE: Well, if everything fails... *(She stands lost in thought for a moment.)* ... then at least if only for a little while I was a stingy millionaire's daughter. I will dress myself up in my coat and hat with my earrings and gloves and parasol – I won't put my gloves on but hold them so my rings can be seen. How I'll dress myself up. So stylish. I'll walk along the streets and down the boulevard and you'll see the great and the small will stare until their eyes burst.

JACHNE-BRAINE: She's stark mad, God knows.

TILLE: Just for a moment to feel like the daughter of a millionaire, to feel that people look at you and run after you.

JACHNE-BRAINE: They run after mad Matilda too. And that's the way they'll run after you.

TILLE: You don't know how wonderful it is. If you could only have been there. How they all looked at me. With such respect. This is the way I walked with my head held high and with an expression...like this... Oh, how well I could act the part of a millionaire's daughter. And you'll see. I'll be one yet.

JACHNE-BRAINE: Well, what do you say to that? Of what are you persuading yourself? Of what?

TILLE: Oh, you don't understand. You don't understand.

JACHNE-BRAINE: And if nothing comes of the whole business, how will you look then? How anxious will you be then to parade yourself in town?

TILLE: Always how and why and wherefore? Go to hell. Let God borrow trouble for the morrow. Today, I'm a millionaire. What a lovely dress I've ordered. I don't know where I get my knowledge of fashion from. I suppose if one has money, one has good taste too.

JACHNE-BRAINE: You could find no better time either to 'fancy up' yourself than a fast day.

TILLE: Didn't the merchants sell me their goods today? For what purpose did they sit in their shops today? If they hadn't been sitting there I might not have bought anything at all. I didn't know whether to spend the money or take it to the bank. But when I passed Seldowitch's and saw in the window Schmerling's daughter's dress at half price, then I said to myself: You only have one life. Where is it written that Tille, the daughter of Chone the gravedigger, must go about like a beggar all her life? What will be, will be. The money has been found whatever happens.

JACHNE-BRAINE: Better if you'd kept quiet about that.

TILLE: Suddenly the desire overcame me to play the part of a millionaire. As simple as that. The thought flashed through my mind, and the shops were open...

JACHNE-BRAINE: You are fasting. Where did you get the strength from...

TILLE: Millionaires don't fast. From the Parisian shop I went to Leon's confectionary and...

JACHNE-BRAINE: May it leap out of your throat. That you had choked on the very first bite. Get out of my sight, blasphemer, or I'll scratch your eyes out. Oh, I – I –

TILLE: *(Laughs.)* How delightful the bonbon was after fasting. Wouldn't you like to eat something too? Come with me and I'll treat you.

JACHNE-BRAINE: May death be visited unto you. Oh my God. May He deliver wounds unto you. Whore!

TILLE: As you please. But come quickly, mother, quickly, and I'll tell you something in confidence. If I wanted to now... I could have a dozen men.

JACHNE-BRAINE: What did I say? That's all she has in her head. Men. Men.

TILLE: Don't you know, mother – it's the main thing.

JACHNE-BRAINE: I curse you and your thoughts. I don't have the strength for you now, otherwise... *(An outer door is heard opening.)* Your father. Back from prayers.

CHONE enters, stick in hand, wearing a worn, greasy black coat over his ritual garment.

CHONE: *(Excitedly.)* What did I say? Didn't I tell you?

He sees TILLE and stands open mouthed.

Behold. Verily. Verily. How she's decked out. *(TILLE laughs. To JACHNE-BRAINE.)* Do you know what she's done? She'll end by ruining us completely.

JACHNE-BRAINE: What is it? What's happened?

CHONE: *(To TILLE.)* I'll rip those things to rags. I'll drive you from the house.

TILLE: Why do you rant so? What have I done that is so terrible?

CHONE: She asks! The peacock! She has blazoned it abroad, told the entire town, that we have found a treasure and she's thrown money around as if... as if it were really true. And now she asks what she has done?

TILLE: Well, as a matter of fact, what?

CHONE: Do you hear her? She asks! You clod with two eyes. You animal with no brain. Black and blue I will beat you.

TILLE: You will, you will. Why don't you sit down, have your tea instead and break your fast.

CHONE: Like you. At the confectioner's?

JACHNE-BRAINE: Even that you know already?

CHONE: What do you think? The whole town is talking of it. Do you think I could pray? Do you think anybody could pray? No one talked of anything else but her and her treasure. Was there anyone who didn't come up to me and pump me for information? The whole synagogue surrounded me. I had to sit on the front bench next to Soskin.

TILLE: Next to wealth. What are you complaining about? Haven't I brought honour upon you? Did you ever dream of sitting in the first row among the rich?

CHONE: I thank you for the honour, my clever daughter. Had you rather broken your neck before you won this honour for me. What am I to do tomorrow when people discover I have found no treasure?

TILLE: Then you can take up your usual station by the door again. But in the meantime, you did sit in the first row next to a rich man. What did you lose by it?

JACHNE-BRAINE: That's what she always asks.

CHONE: I could well have done without sitting in the first row. Do you understand? Why did you have to prattle? Why did you have to run off suddenly and deck yourself out and eat at the confectioner's and ride in a cab? What right had you to the money?

TILLE: We settled that before.

CHONE: Settled? How settled? Who settled it? You will come up with all the money yet! You will carry all those things back and bring me the money.

TILLE: You tell them, Judke. The money is mine, isn't it?

JUDKE: Gave it you...to you...all...

CHONE: But I'll...

JACHNE-BRAINE: Chone, you forget you've been fasting. Go and wash your hands and eat. Have a glass of tea. *(She pours.)* Oh, oh. I can hardly move my limbs. This business. A fine addition on top of our fasting.

CHONE: I've had enough for now. All this excitement has taken it out of me. *(He sits and drinks.)* And besides, the sexton brought whisky and cakes after prayers. We drank – the Rabbi and Soskin and the President of the Congregation...

TILLE: You see? Do you see? You owe me that too.

CHONE: And I won't fail to repay you, either. You'll feel my gratitude in your bones. Yes, if it were true, if I really had the treasure, what would I have cared? But how will I face the world tomorrow? Why did you have to blab? It grew dark before my eyes when I heard them talking of the treasure. First I thought, they know we haven't found it yet...

TILLE: And you thought, of course, the whole town will rush to the cemetery to look for it.

CHONE: My arms and legs were paralysed with fear. And when I heard them speak of the treasure already being found, I wanted to deny it, to swear there was nothing. But they told me it was too late. My little daughter... Oh, that I may be delivered from her soon.

TILLE: Amen.

CHONE: Be silent, or...

TILLE: I mean, you ought to marry me off soon. Why do you grow so angry?

CHONE: Marry you off? Yes, to death. They told me my little daughter had spent a handsome sum for clothes and jewels in the very best shops. I opened my mouth and my ears. I didn't know anything about it. All I know about is a few coins and not even how many because my dear daughter pocketed the lot. May the devil pocket you.

JACHNE-BRAINE: Amen.

CHONE: So I said, I know there were ten to fifteen sovereigns, perhaps fewer. But they laughed. You don't know how to lie, Reb Chone, they said. Reb Chone, that's what they said. Not just Chone.

TILLE: Hurrah.

CHONE: *(Throwing her an angry glance.)* There's no use lying, they said. Your daughter spent twice that much today. I didn't know, of course, what to say to that. I stammered and stuttered and they all wished me happiness and squeezed my hand and I stood there and I didn't know whether I was dreaming or had gone mad. And then the Rabbi said he had something to consult me about.

TILLE: *(Loud laughter.)* He wants you to side with him against the other Rabbi who has been sent for.

CHONE: And then came Soskin and wanted to consult me too.

JACHNE-BRAINE: Ah, the morsels will stick in my throat.

TILLE: I suppose he wants you to be his partner. Ha, ha, ha.

CHONE: I wish I knew what to say to them as I know what I think of you. *(Cries out.)* I'd like to tear you to pieces. What have you brought upon me?

TILLE laughs.

JACHNE-BRAINE: And she laughs.

TILLE: Isn't it funny? We are…

CHONE: *(In a rage.)* Oh! *(He takes a step towards her but restrains himself.)* Tell me at once how much money you had.

TILLE: More, at all events, than I have now.

CHONE: Speak plainly.

JACHNE-BRAINE: Why won't you tell us?

TILLE: Because the money is mine and I don't have to account for it to you. Also, it's more interesting if you don't know.

JACHNE-BRAINE: What do you say to that?

CHONE: Wait. I'll make you speak fast enough. *(He picks up the stick.)* Will you speak?

JUDKE: *(Bleating malevolently.)* Hay, hay, hay.

JACHNE-BRAINE: Let us at least finish eating.

TILLE: *(Calmly.)* You'd better not lose any time in useless debate. Eat and then let us go and find the treasure.

37

CHONE: At once you are to tell me.

TILLE: Very well. I'll give you what you want. If nothing comes of the treasure, I'll tell you exactly how many coins there were.

CHONE: *(Beats the floor with his stick.)* I want to know it now. You are to tell me at once. I must know what I am to say to people tomorrow...

TILLE: Are you really going to tell them the truth?

CHONE: What I'm going to say doesn't concern you. How much money did you have?

TILLE: What you see accounts for all that I had.

CHONE: How many sovereigns?

TILLE: Fifteen.

CHONE: Twenty?

TILLE: Twenty.

CHONE: *(Rushes at her.)* Are you mocking me?

JACHNE-BRAINE: *(Holding him back.)* You see she won't tell.

JUDKE: Don't tell.

CHONE: She'll tell soon enough.

JACHNE-BRAINE: Wait a day or two until we know about the treasure. You had better sit down and eat. Oh God above, God above.

TILLE: That's my advice too.

JACHNE-BRAINE: Stop talking.

TILLE: We must hurry up and eat and go out to look. The night is clear. And I'm hungry too. At the confectioner's I just nibbled dainties.

She sits at the table.

CHONE: *(Calmer but with a glance full of hatred and contempt.)* On a fast day at the confectioner's. I'm a fool to lay aside the stick.

He exits to the outer hall.

TILLE: After the bonbons, this horseradish tastes sickly.

JACHNE-BRAINE: She has become a gourmet suddenly, the millionairess.

CHONE enters with wet hands, dries them, pronounces the blessing, sits and eats.

TILLE: How good the ice cream tasted.

JACHNE-BRAINE: Be quiet. Don't provoke him.

CHONE: And the stuff didn't choke you.

TILLE: As you see.

They eat. Silence.

CHONE: She just went away and made her purchases. What all did she buy?

TILLE: Now that's a different way of talking.

JACHNE-BRAINE: She bought quite enough.

TILLE: *(Jumps up, smoothes her dress, places her hands on her hips and swings round in front of CHONE.)* Look. Stylish, eh? *(Shows him the rings.)* And – *(Shakes her earrings.)* and – *(Shows the watch and chain.)* and – *(Puts on the hat.)*. And this. *(Opens the parasol.)* Well, how does your firstborn please you now? *(She spreads out the cloak.)* And then this – *(She throws it across her shoulders and assumes the air of a fashionable lady.)*

CHONE: Did you ever see such a pretentious carry on.

TILLE: If we can find the treasure you'll see what I can really make of myself. Look what I bought the rest of you. Cloth. To make suits for you and Judke and a dress for mother. Look at the quality.

CHONE: *(Glances angrily at the cloth then turns away.)* And the diamonds are real?

TILLE: What? Am I likely to buy paste? Your only daughter doesn't wear paste.

JACHNE-BRAINE: Don't make such a fuss. Sit down and let us finish this joyous meal.

CHONE: *(Having finished his meal.)* Well, we have a fine daughter – finer than you can say. She does as she pleases. Her parents have to get on as best they can in spite of her.

JACHNE-BRAINE shakes her head.

TILLE: Let's first find the treasure. Then everything will be well. Then I'll call you 'papa'.

CHONE: He hasn't remembered yet?

JACHNE-BRAINE: You expect him to? Do you? You can wait a long time.

CHONE: *(Groans.)* Aaah. *(To JUDKE.)* Were there many coins?

JUDKE: *(Who has been staring at the table while the others ate.)* Won't tell. Won't talk to you.

CHONE: I'll get you to talk.

He mumbles the post-prandial prayer.

JACHNE-BRAINE: Crazy Judke.

TILLE: What do you want to eat?

JUDKE: Want nothing.

TILLE: Were there more coins?

JUDKE: Don't remember nothing.

TILLE: Shame. Schutschke was such a good doggy, and not even to know where he's buried.

JUDKE: *(Beats his head with his fist.)* Why don't I remember? Why don't I remember?

TILLE: Don't act crazy. Have a good sleep and then you'll remember.

JUDKE sits for a while then gets up, takes the roll of cloth, goes to the bench and stretches out on it. He giggles and caresses the cloth, then falls asleep. CHONE finishes the prayer. Knocking.

JACHNE-BRAINE: Someone's coming.

The Marriage Broker enters.

MARRIAGE BROKER: Good evening. May your fast agree with you.

JACHNE-BRAINE and CHONE: *(Surprised.)* Good evening.

TILLE: Good evening! What a guest!

JACHNE-BRAINE: To think of the matchmaker finding his way to us, and such a grand one too.

MARRIAGE BROKER: A man puts off finding his way to the cemetery as long as is possible. Ha, ha, ha.

JACHNE-BRAINE: And so the gravedigger's daughter must be an old maid.

TILLE: She isn't old yet.

MARRIAGE BROKER: My opinion exactly. What a hot day it has been and what a difficult fast. But that's our Jewish fate. On the longest and hottest days we must fast.

CHONE: We fast in winter too.

MARRIAGE BROKER: I think the summer fast days are superfluous, and yet when does a Jew not suffer hunger? He suffers it continually, thank God, in summer and in winter, on long days and short.

CHONE: A Jew suffers no hunger, except when he has something to eat.

JACHNE-BRAINE: Yes, yes.

She begins to clear the table. She carries the plates into the kitchen, puts the bread in a cupboard, shakes the tablecloth in a corner and replaces it on the table.

MARRIAGE BROKER: Did you have a busy day today?

CHONE: We never lack work on any day.

MARRIAGE BROKER: People die regardless.

CHONE: And without self-control. Today we had four buryings and this week we...

MARRIAGE BROKER: Yes, yes, people die. But God sends the balm before the hurt is felt. He has supplied the world with marriage brokers who see to it that the young are united so they can beget children, and so the whole business keeps turning.

TILLE: Then a marriage broker is finer than a gravedigger.

MARRIAGE BROKER: The best thing of all is to get married oneself.

TILLE: That depends.

MARRIAGE BROKER: *(Takes a cigarette and hands the case to CHONE.)* Help yourself, Reb Chone. Well, the things one hears about you. *(Laughs. The two men smoke.)*

CHONE: I see you've already heard something.

MARRIAGE BROKER: Naturally. The whole town is buzzing with it. *(Jachne Braine sighs.)* So that's your daughter. And you have only the one?

JACHNE-BRAINE: That you might have found out long ago.

MARRIAGE BROKER: You must understand me and not take it ill. A marriage broker is not a gravedigger. He profits by the living and not by the dead. And poor people are like the dead, ha, ha, ha.

TILLE: So poor girls don't get married?

MARRIAGE BROKER: Understand me. I'm a marriage broker who – you mustn't misunderstand me or feel hurt –who has arranged some majestic matches and in the wealthiest of families. I represent young men who are worth five — ten – twenty thousand roubles and more. I have doctors and lawyers and engineers and some fine young men, highly educated, who possess fortunes of their own. Now, I am looking for a wife for a chemist...

JACHNE-BRAINE: For a what?

MARRIAGE BROKER: A chemist, a smart, erudite man. You must have heard of Shalom Balashkin's son. A head he has on him. You won't find his equal. He's an inventor and people are offering him hundreds of thousands for a... for a kind of new colour he's made. But he doesn't want to sell. He wants to build his own factory to produce the colour himself and in two or three years he'll be a millionaire. That's the kind of colour it is. To do this, he needs – you understand me – twenty-five thousand roubles. And since he has no money of his own he's looking for a wife with such a dowry.

TILLE: Is he handsome?

MARRIAGE BROKER: Who? The chemist? Handsome? Suppose he isn't? Is that so important? The main thing about a man is that he can earn a great deal of money.

TILLE: If I'm to give a dowry of twenty-five thousand I won't have anyone who isn't handsome.

MARRIAGE BROKER: All girls make the same mistake. A handsome man is nothing special. A handsome man is far too vain and, the way things are today, you have to keep an eye on him wherever he goes. The main thing is here. *(He taps his head.)*

TILLE: No. The main thing for me is looks. I'll make him keep an eye on me and not the other way round.

MARRIAGE BROKER: Look at her. She has grown up here...

TILLE: If I have a dowry of twenty-five thousand, he needn't bother his brain too much.

MARRIAGE BROKER: He'll be a millionaire soon. Another man might waste your money and you'll not know where it's gone.

TILLE: I'd rather be poor – if he's handsome.

MARRIAGE BROKER: Well, then, I must tell you – and you mustn't take it amiss – that you talk just like a child.

TILLE: What shall I do if he's ugly and loses the money as well? What then? I'd have nothing to eat and nothing to look at.

MARRIAGE BROKER: Loses the money? They're offering him hundreds of thousands.

TILLE: Have you only one on your list?

MARRIAGE BROKER: What? Only one? May we find as many treasures as I have young men on my list. And handsome! I'm only talking about the chemist because...

TILLE: The handsome ones, with fiery black eyes...

MARRIAGE BROKER: I have one like that too. An engineer. But let us speak plainly. *(To CHONE.)* How much dowry are you going to give?

CHONE: I – dowry?

JACHNE-BRAINE: We – dowry?

TILLE: It depends on the young man.

MARRIAGE BROKER: Five, ten, twenty – fifty thousand? They're saying the treasure's worth maybe a million.

JACHNE-BRAINE: Huh. May all the evil in the world overwhelm my enemies.

CHONE: Truly, I feel sick when people begin to talk of it.

MARRIAGE BROKER: What other people have always looks more than it is, you know. People say a million. I suppose it is less. But how much less? We know what is meant by treasure.

A treasure is not a small affair. I really think you might be frank with me. However much you have may it be a source of nothing but good for you. On this day you were destined to find treasure and find treasure you did. On another day, good fortune may come to me and I'll find a fortune. Ha, ha. Far from envying you, I'm very glad that you found it and not another man, perhaps a childless one. Through you at least I can earn a little. A daughter you have, and a son too, though people say he's a cripple. Is that him on the bench? Well, we'll manage to provide for him too. It'll be harder perhaps. The main thing I want to know is – the price. What does it cost? You understand me? In short, tell me how much you will give and then we'll be ready.

JACHNE-BRAINE: Oh dear, oh dear me.

CHONE: Tell me. Do you know what you're talking about?

MARRIAGE BROKER: I understand, I understand. Don't, be upset. In your position I would act just the same. Do you think I would rush into town and cry out: I have found so much? Huh? I wouldn't dream of it. In a trice I'd have the whole town down about my ears, everyone wanting something and pulling at my pocket... I would be silent too, as sure as sure as I have breath in my body. And if I were to say anything I'd make it ten or twenty times less than it is. But as between us. A very different matter. Keep your money all you want, but let me know how much dowry you're going to give your daughter.

TILLE: I've already told you. It depends, and he must be handsome.

CHONE: Am I crazy or are you?

JACHNE-BRAINE: Dear oh dear.

MARRIAGE BROKER: I see it is with your daughter I must speak.

CHONE: May I know as little of any evil as I know of what's going on here.

MARRIAGE BROKER: You'll have to marry off your daughter. You're not going to lock her up in a cell. And it strikes me she wouldn't let you. The sooner you marry her off, the better.

CHONE: But...

JACHNE-BRAINE: Oh my dear God.

MARRIAGE BROKER: If you think another marriage broker would find better matches you are greatly mistaken. I believe you know what matches I have been responsible for. You need not be ashamed to have me suggest a suitable match for your daughter.

CHONE: God in heaven, what a torment.

JACHNE-BRAINE: As I live.

MARRIAGE BROKER: Who is a torment? No one has ever said that to me before and I am welcome in the best Jewish houses. It's clear I'm dealing here with paupers who have just grown rich. Do you know what I say to you? I don't believe in the treasure any more. A handsome treasure it's likely to be – a sovereign and a half, perhaps.

CHONE: Don't believe in the treasure, I tell you! Don't believe in it!

TILLE has risen, smoothed her frock, extended her hand with the rings on and turned her head to make the earrings sparkle.

MARRIAGE BROKER: A torment. As though I'd come to beg for alms.

TILLE: Don't be annoyed. Discuss the matter with me.

MARRIAGE BROKER: The sum! I must know the sum! Is it...

TILLE: Five, ten, fifty, a hundred thousand –

CHONE: Wha-at?

JACHNE-BRAINE opens her mouth and sits as if petrified.

MARRIAGE BROKER: That's clear but what happens if your father won't give that much?

TILLE: Rely on me. He'll come round.

MARRIAGE BROKER: I see one may depend on you. You wear the trousers round here, eh? Now, what shall I do? Shall I wire?

TILLE: Yes, you may wire. But I want none but the handsome, mind.

MARRIAGE BROKER: You may rely upon me. Handsome as a picture. Exceptional. You won't grow tired of looking at him. It's this very engineer. But it can't be managed for less than thirty thousand.

TILLE: Even if it takes fifty thousand he must be handsome.

CHONE: *(Clutching his head.)* Aa-ah.

MARRIAGE BROKER: Tall and strong. Like a guardsman. With black fiery eyes.

TILLE: *(With faltering breath.)* You may telegraph. Does he live far?

MARRIAGE BROKER: If I wire now he could be here tomorrow night at eleven.

TILLE: Then go and wire...

MARRIAGE BROKER: I just wanted to tell you of his good family line, but I am going to wire right away. Money for the telegram please.

TILLE: Certainly.

She exits to the other room.

MARRIAGE BROKER: She's got good sense for sure. She won't have to guard her husband.

CHONE and JACHNE-BRAINE sit with open mouths as if bereft of their senses. TILLE returns and gives the broker a bank note.

TILLE: There. It won't cost as much. The rest is for your trouble.

MARRIAGE BROKER: She knows how to behave. She herself will be a treasure to her husband, regardless of a dowry. I'll hurry now. Good night to you all. May I come back later and discuss the matter fully?

TILLE: Not necessary. One must rest after a fast. The main thing is that he pleases me.

MARRIAGE BROKER: She's clever, sure as I have breath in my body. You'll see how handsome he is. Good night.

He goes. Brief pause.

TILLE: *(Breaking out laughing, claps her hands and dances.)* Millionairess. A millionairess. It's working. The trick is working.

CHONE: If I don't have a stroke it's only because I'm stronger than iron.

JACHNE-BRAINE: It'll drive us mad. What kind of joke is this?

CHONE: It's enough. Now I want to know how much money you have. *(To JACHNE BRAINE.)* Who knows? Perhaps she really has a million? *(To TILLE.)* You'll tell me at once how much you have, do you hear? You won't escape me this time. *(To JACHNE BRAINE.)* Why did she go out before? Where does she keep the money?

JACHNE-BRAINE: How do I know?

TILLE: A millionairess. I'm a millionairess. You don't understand a joke.

CHONE: I'll strip you naked. I'll tear every last shred off your back. This minute you'll hand over the money.

TILLE: What money? I've told you I haven't any.

CHONE: You expect me to believe that? Where did you get that five roubles you gave the matchmaker? All your talk to him – was that just a joke?

TILLE: If it was a joke, so what? The main thing…

CHONE: Don't try to confuse me. Put the money down here. I don't even want to take it away from you. I just want to look at it. To see how money looks. All my life I have seen no real money. I just want a glimpse...

JACHNE-BRAINE: I don't even know my own daughter.

Someone is heard at the door.

TILLE: Keep still. A visitor to the owner of the treasure.

CHONE: *(Whispering between his teeth.)* Just wait. You'll give me that money yet.

SOSKIN enters. He's short sighted, well dressed, self-important.

SOSKIN: Good evening.

CHONE: *(Jumps up, surprised, embarrassed.)* Now look at this... Mr Soskin. Good evening.

Behind SOSKIN's back, JACHNE-BRAINE clasps her hands, frightened, astonished. TILLE bites her lip to avoid laughing.

SOSKIN: A difficult fast, wasn't it?

He takes a chair and makes himself comfortable.

CHONE: Yes, a fast day as ever.

He sits slowly. TILLE picks up a book and sits. JACHNE-BRAINE doesn't dare sit.

SOSKIN: Were there many funerals today?

CHONE: No lack of them on any day, thank God.

SOSKIN: And today you have dug *up* something also.

CHONE looks stupefied. TILLE raises her eyes but lowers them immediately and smiles. JACHNE-BRAINE looks at CHONE, then at TILLE meaningfully, shakes her head angrily and sighs.

Where did you dig it up? The old field or the new?

CHONE: *(Smiles in great embarrassment.)* Hmmm.

SOSKIN: As I asked you in the synagogue, and, if I am not mistaken, you said the new...

CHONE: Yes? How could I have said that?

SOSKIN: I don't know but that is what you said.

CHONE: May I know as little of any evil as I know of having said that.

SOSKIN: I don't understand why you should be so afraid or why you seem to regret what you said.

CHONE: Regret? How can I regret saying what I couldn't have said.

SOSKIN: Why couldn't you have said it? If you found it in the new field, well and good, you found it there.

JACHNE-BRAINE: Oh father above, father above.

SOSKIN: How many burials did you say you had?

CHONE: Four.

SOSKIN: Where?

CHONE: In the...

SOSKIN: *(As if he hadn't heard.)* Where?

CHONE: *(At a loss, turns to wife and daughter.)* Where? Where did I?

JACHNE-BRAINE: There you are. He asks me!

TILLE: The old field – it seems to me.

SOSKIN: *(Laughs.)* The old field. It seems. Why do you ask her anyway? You did the burying. You're the one who knows. But the matter can be discovered. Isn't that so, Reb Chone. All we have to do is look into the records and then we would know at once...

TILLE: Why do you have to know at all?

SOSKIN: *(Disregarding the question.)* Even a blind man can see you dug graves in the new field today, otherwise you would

50

have told me at once and not first consulted your wife and daughter.

TILLE: Yes, but how does it concern you so much?

SOSKIN: How concern me? Oh, not at all. I'm just surprised at your desire to conceal the truth. If you found treasure in the new field, why don't you simply say so.

TILLE: But it does seem to matter to you. A great deal. Otherwise you wouldn't have taken the trouble to come here so late on a fast day and ask Chone the gravedigger where he found his treasure.

SOSKIN: In respectable homes, children don't interfere.

TILLE: *(Mutters.)* If our family isn't respectable, you needn't marry into it.

CHONE: Hold your tongue.

JACHNE-BRAINE: She should be burned.

SOSKIN: *(To CHONE.)* Can't we go into another room and discuss this properly?

TILLE: *(Lays her book aside.)* You don't have to talk to father at all. I found the treasure, not him.

SOSKIN: You must first make me believe that.

TILLE: You needn't believe it if you don't want to.

SOSKIN: *(To CHONE.)* I'd still like to talk to you alone.

CHONE: If you want to know the whole truth, I swear that I found nothing at all.

SOSKIN: Who did then?

TILLE: Haven't you been told?

SOSKIN: What business has she to be digging around on a grave?

CHONE: Ask her. How do I know? There she sits. Let her tell you.

SOSKIN: Which means you've agreed between you not to tell.

CHONE: Why did we need to agree?

JACHNE-BRAINE: Oh God, oh God.

SOSKIN: I don't know. I wasn't listening behind the door.

TILLE: But you've agreed with yourself that we made the find in the new field and you want to insist on persuading us it was there. So you must have some interest in the matter.

SOSKIN: All I know is this. In the synagogue you said clearly and unmistakably that you found the treasure yourself in the new field.

CHONE: How come? I don't even know where anything was found.

SOSKIN: You are denying everything you said. How will it be when I bring forward witnesses?

TILLE: Witnesses?

SOSKIN: I'll tell you what to do. Show me the hole where the treasure was found.

TILLE: It's been filled in long ago.

SOSKIN: Why?

TILLE: So a blind horse wouldn't fall in.

SOSKIN: *(Jumps up.)* Let me tell you then that you have a lawsuit on your hands.

CHONE: A lawsuit.

JACHNE-BRAINE: I die.

TILLE: What kind of lawsuit?

SOSKIN: *(Going to the door.)* You'll learn in good time.

TILLE: I get it. The Congregation bought the new field from him. That's why he insists we found the treasure there. *(Laughs.)* Don't you understand? He wants a share.

SOSKIN: If not all of it. Well, if you've found so much common sense . . .

TILLE: It's just occurred to me. It didn't at first. A share is what he wants.

SOSKIN: You found the treasure in the new field. I sold the field to the Congregation but not what was buried in it.

TILLE: But you didn't bury the treasure yourself. You knew nothing of it.

SOSKIN: A proper little lawyer, aren't we. But I am as well informed in these matters of law as you are. You will have to turn every kopek over to me or . . .

TILLE: Or?

SOSKIN: You will all be taken away to prison.

CHONE: What a visitation has come upon us.

JACHNE-BRAINE: I can't bear any more.

TILLE: Is that so? To prison? I'd like to see you try.

SOSKIN: You will believe it in good time.

JACHNE-BRAINE: Oh God above. What a misfortune. What kind of treasure do we have? Where is any treasure? For the love of God.

SOSKIN: You want to deny the whole business? You want to act as though you haven't found any treasure worth several hundred thousands if not more?

CHONE: Several hundred thousands?

He looks wildly at TILLE.

TILLE: Go ahead. Start your lawsuit. We are as rich as you and quite as able to hire a lawyer. We will prove beyond any reasonable doubt that we didn't find the treasure in the new field. Go ahead now. We'll see who comes out on top.

SOSKIN: I have witnesses . . .

CHONE: But I couldn't...

TILLE: It's all right. Let him be. Let him produce his witnesses in court. And if you did say it? What of it? You lied. That's all. You didn't want to tell them the truth.

CHONE: But I didn't say it... I couldn't...

JACHNE-BRAINE: How is it he couldn't...

SOSKIN: You'll see where your daughter will land you. Good night.

He goes toward the door.

CHONE: For the love of God. Did anyone hear of such things.

JACHNE-BRAINE: *(Bursting into tears.)* What a mess, what a mess.

SOSKIN: *(At the door, turns.)* Why don't we make a bargain, like decent Jews, without law suits or courts? I know for certain you found the treasure in the new field.

TILLE: Not true.

SOSKIN: If you should undertake to prove that, you will bring great misery upon yourselves. For perjury you go to prison.

TILLE: Your witnesses are the ones who'll be perjuring themselves.

SOSKIN: Wouldn't it be better to sort this out amongst ourselves and with generous hearts?

TILLE: Useless chatter. You can go on talking till dusk tomorrow. It won't make the treasure be found in the new field.

JACHNE-BRAINE: *(In tears.)* What treasure? What kind of treasure?

CHONE: It's enough to drive you mad.

SOSKIN: So you don't want to agree on a compromise?

TILLE: Not for a kopek.

SOSKIN: Now I ask you, Reb Chone, you're an old man – would you rather become involved in lawsuits or a compromise?

CHONE: But I don't know anything at all. I have found no…

SOSKIN: I advise you. It would be better to compromise.

TILLE: Ha, ha, ha.

CHONE: But I didn't…

SOSKIN: Very well. We'll meet at a different place. Think it over carefully. That's all. Good night.

He leaves. TILLE laughs.

CHONE: I'll beat you to death and worse. Did I not say that she would plunge us into misery. She'll finish us.

JACHNE-BRAINE: She'll get us all sent to gaol.

CHONE: And still she laughs. Look what she has done. All because she suddenly took a fancy to prettying herself up.

JACHNE-BRAINE: And considers no one else. Does as she pleases.

CHONE: What do you say to such misfortune? Treasure! They cry treasure. And I know nothing. Except for the five sovereigns, I haven't seen anything. I don't know where and I don't know what.

TILLE: Then laugh with me. What frightens you so?

CHONE: God above. May death shake you to the core. Am I not to be frightened? That man will have me gaoled.

TILLE: What for? Did you find the treasure? Do you even know where Judke found the sovereigns?

CHONE: Perhaps it really was a treasure. You see how excited the town is. 'Hundreds of thousands, perhaps more.' How do I know? Maybe you showed that much money.

TILLE: *(Laughs.)* What a joke.

Someone is heard arriving.

JACHNE-BRAINE: *(Weakened by emotion.)* Hold on. Someone else is coming.

The PRESIDENT of the Congregation enters.

PRESIDENT: Good evening.

CHONE: *(Depressed.)* Good evening.

JACHNE-BRAINE: *(Sighs.)* Another one.

TILLE turns away and laughs. The PRESIDENT sits.

PRESIDENT: I have come, Reb Chone, direct from the Council. It has convened in extraordinary session. You will easily guess what was under discussion.

CHONE: *(So weary he can scarcely speak.)* I can guess.

PRESIDENT: Why do you sigh, Reb Chone. God has shown you his especial favour. And since you understand that the Congregation desires a share from you . . .

CHONE: A share of what? A share from who?

PRESIDENT: Let me explain. Today you have found a treasure of many thousands, of hundreds of thousands . . .

JACHNE-BRAINE tears her hair. CHONE stares wildly at TILLE.

When a man has so suddenly been favoured by God it is but meet that he should think of the Congregation too. The more he gives away of what God has given him, the more blessed will he be. But your case is different.

CHONE: Oh God above.

PRESIDENT: Don't sigh, Reb Chone. The Congregation is no thief. The Congregation demands only what is just. You yourself realise the treasure was found on land owned by the Congregation and that you yourself are a servant of the Congregation. On the basis of these facts, the Congregation might even demand you hand over the entire sum but as I have said, the Congregation does not want to rob you. So, the Council has decided you should divide the treasure with the Congregation, a share each. Isn't that just?

CHONE: *(Moaning.)* I don't know any longer what to say.

TILLE: Father had a very hard fast today and also they gave him whisky in the synagogue...

PRESIDENT: Shall we put off our discussion until tomorrow?

CHONE: I don't know anything.

JACHNE-BRAINE: We're going crazy.

PRESIDENT: Very well. Until tomorrow, though I should prefer to sort it out without delay.

TILLE: You've held your Council. We should like a chance to think it over too.

PRESIDENT: What is there to think over? Surely you'll not set yourself against the Congregation?

TILLE: Nevertheless, we must think it over. Father can hardly speak.

PRESIDENT: Very well. We'll let it go until tomorrow. But I might as well tell you, Reb Chone, that the Congregation will insist on its share and will not bargain over it. Furthermore, I must warn you not to hide any part of the treasure and then pretend to have a smaller sum than you have found. That would be committing theft against the Congregation and the members of the Council could not tolerate that.

TILLE: We are as honest as other people are.

PRESIDENT: So much the better. *(He rises.)* Good night. You will be good enough to come over to the Council tomorrow morning. We'll expect you immediately after prayers. Good night.

CHONE: *(Utterly downcast.)* I'd like to speak out and – good night.

JACHNE-BRAINE: Good night. *(Sighs.)*

The PRESIDENT goes.

CHONE: *(To TILLE.)* What have you to say now? What have you to say?

TILLE: What is there to say? They have smelled money...

JACHNE-BRAINE: Money, you say. I'm smelling the misery that will befall us.

CHONE: What am I to tell the Council?

TILLE: If you want to be very generous, give them half.

CHONE: Look. She laughs. She mocks me. That half of what am I to give them? Half of five sovereigns? *(TILLE laughs.)* She's heartless.

JACHNE-BRAINE: May she be laughing for the last time, oh God above.

CHONE: They'll do to me I don't know what. Do you think they'll believe me if I tell them the truth? She buys diamonds and watches and God only knows what for how much money. To the matchmaker she says 'a hundred thousand roubles'. To Soskin she says 'We are as rich as you'. And then I will go and lay down five sovereigns on the table and say 'Here is my treasure and I am kind enough to share it with you'

TILLE: *(Laughs.)* Well, that wouldn't be a lie.

CHONE: This is too much. *(Cries out in a violent rage as if possessed.)* I'll kill you. I'll beat you to pulp. What do you want of me? Why do you drive me mad? Eh? Oh, I'll – where is my stick? Where? *(He grabs his stick.)* Hand it over. All of it. Now.

JUDKE wakes and looks in astonishment at his father.

TILLE: All the money.

CHONE: Yes. All of it, the hundreds of thousands, the entire million. I won't wait another second.

TILLE: Hundreds of thousands. There, Judke is awake.
Ask him how many coins he brought home.

CHONE: I don't want to know. Just give me all the money
you have on you now.

TILLE: It's under my corset.

CHONE: Then untie your stays and give it to me.

TILLE: If that's what you want.

She undoes her corset.

JUDKE: Tille, I've slept but I don't remember.

TILLE: *(To CHONE.)* I tell you it's my money I'm giving you.
(She pulls out a few crumpled notes and drops them on the table.) Here.
The entire amount, the hundreds of thousands, the million.

CHONE: *(Throws himself upon the notes, counts them with a trembling
hand and cries out.)* Thirty-five roubles.

He turns the notes over. JACHNE-BRAINE helps him.

TILLE: *(Doing up her corset.)* Looking won't make any more
appear.

CHONE: *(Throwing the notes back on the table.)* I don't believe you.
You've taken...

TILLE: Do you want to strip me down to my skin?

CHONE: What kind of a comedy did you play with the
matchmaker then?

TILLE: Why should you be upset because I have fun?
I didn't call him. He came of his own accord. He thinks
we've grown rich. Let him go ahead. Why should you
worry?

JACHNE-BRAINE: A fine way of having fun. Tomorrow night
at eleven the bridegroom will come...

TILLE: What have you to lose if he does? If we find the
treasure, all's well. If not, I'll say the engineer doesn't suit

me. Then I become an old maid once more and he goes back home.

CHONE: And if Soskin sues me?

JACHNE-BRAINE: Oh my God.

CHONE: And what shall I say to the Council? *(Scratches his head.)* Oh, oh, oh.

JUDKE: *(Comes from the bench.)* I go look.

He goes out.

TILLE: Follow him. Hurry.

CHONE: What's the use?

TILLE: He gives up so soon. What if there is treasure?

CHONE: Do you think I have strength enough left to move anywhere?

TILLE: I'm sorry. Only it's a pity. The night is so clear and bright. I'll just change my clothes and then I'll go myself.

She takes down a dress hanging against the wall and goes into the next room.

CHONE: Well, there you sit like a lady of leisure.

JACHNE-BRAINE: Much strength have I to move. I can barely stand on my two feet after such a fast day.

CHONE: And what about me? My head is swimming. Let's go together. I'm about to fall over.

JACHNE-BRAINE: May my enemies feel as much pain as this. Come on, then. Come on.

CHONE: Ah.

They drag themselves to the door. CHONE remembers the money lying on the table, turns round, puts the notes in his pocket and sighs. They exit. TILLE enters with her old dress on and the new one over her arm. She looks about.

TILLE: They went after all. Both of them.

She strokes the new dress, looks at it, brushes off a speck of dust, hums to herself, finds it hard to leave it but finally hangs it up under the sheet against the wall. She admires her hat and takes it with her parasol and gloves into the next room. She returns at once and, still humming, looks at her earrings in the mirror. She cries out.

A millionairess at least for a day.

She hurries out.

SCENE 3

Same room. Next morning. Dull. It's raining. Bedding is lying on the sofa still. CHONE gets out his prayer shawl. JACHNE-BRAINE, JUDKE and TILLE, in her accustomed state of early undress but bejewelled, sit at the table and drink tea. A samovar stands on the table. JACHNE-BRAINE groans heavily. CHONE murmurs his prayers, then stops.

CHONE: There you are. I have to pray at home. I daren't go to the synagogue. I must hide. All on account of her madness. May she break her neck in two.

TILLE: On an empty stomach he unloads his curses. And he calls that praying.

CHONE: May you be unloaded from this world. If it were not for you I wouldn't have fallen upon this evil. One thing I ask. I've hidden my face, and I won't go to the Council but what shall I do if they summon me?

TILLE: Don't go. That's all.

CHONE: Not go. What do you mean? When the Council summons?

TILLE: Don't be at home when they come.

CHONE: How shall I not be at home? Where in the world am I to be? Can I hide in the earth?

TILLE: You can sit in there. *(Points to the next room.)* Or with the coffins. We will say you've gone away.

CHONE: I can hide from a messenger but if the Council comes. What then? What am I to say?

TILLE: I have a plan. You needn't hide. You needn't avoid the messenger. You needn't do anything. Just pretend to be ill.

CHONE: Ill.

JUDKE bursts out laughing.

JACHNE-BRAINE: *(To TILLE.)* May you really fall ill. Oh God above.

CHONE: What do you mean ill? How can I make myself ill all of a sudden?

JUDKE laughs again.

TILLE: Quite easily. You lie on your bed or on the sofa, and you cover yourself. If anyone comes, we say you're ill. It happens. We'll say you've caught a cold or that fasting didn't agree with you or, simply, that the excitement was too much.

JACHNE-BRAINE: It's truly enough to make anyone ill.

TILLE: If anyone talks to you, you must be quiet and act as though you don't understand or can't hear – or can't speak. Let them talk to the walls. If an answer has to be given, I'll give it.

JACHNE-BRAINE: May your tongue be struck with the stiffness of death.

TILLE: A great piece of good fortune will come to you, mother.

CHONE: So this is how she will make a fool of all the world. But I must ask you. How will it all end? Very well, I grant you I pretend to be ill and I'm lying in bed but I can't spend my life lying in bed. I have to get up some time.

TILLE: We must gain time. Meanwhile, we look for the treasure again.

JACHNE-BRAINE: She'll look for the treasure. In this rain. A sin to drive a dog onto the streets in such weather.

TILLE: To dig graves in the rain, in the snow, in the frost, all for a pittance, you think that's right, eh? You two can stay here. No one asks you to go. Judke and I will go and look. We'll wrap up well and if we do get wet, we won't care, will we?

JUDKE: You go. Me too.

TILLE: You know how important it is.

CHONE: All I want to know is: what will happen afterwards?

TILLE: When exactly?

CHONE: When we've found nothing.

TILLE: Why should we find nothing?

JUDKE: I'll remember. I'll remember.

JACHNE-BRAINE: Oh yes, he's going to remember. May his head be as crooked on his neck as his mind is.

JUDKE: I'll remember, to spite you.

CHONE: Suppose you do find Schutschke's grave, who's to say they'll be any money there?

TILLE: If it comes to the worst, you have the five sovereigns, and the thirty-five roubles. Aren't you almost rich? When did you ever have so much money before?

CHONE: But why did you have to rush out and spend it?

TILLE: You shouldn't have shouted at me. If I've made a mess of things, it can't be helped now. I didn't imagine people would come so quickly wanting things. We need to gain time...

CHONE: Is that the door again?

TILLE: Lie down on the sofa. Quick. Hurry. Lie down.

CHONE stretches out on the sofa.

JACHNE-BRAINE: Oh God above, God above.

TILLE: *(Pause. Goes to the door. Looks out.)* No one there. Only the wind.

CHONE: *(Sits up.)* A fine praying this will be. At every creak I have to lie down with my shawl and...

TILLE: Go to the chamber of rest and pray there.

CHONE: What have you brought down on us?

JACHNE-BRAINE: And I, can I bear it in this room? Drink your tea first. I'll bring you something to eat.

Hands CHONE a glass of tea. TILLE stands on the bed, takes down her new dress and tries it on.

And what's the meaning of this? Rubbing salt in our wounds?

TILLE: I only want to try it on once more. Doesn't it fit like a glove? This button will have to be moved a bit, don't you think? It's a little too full here. *(Turns and looks at herself from different angles.)* If you want something good you have to go to the big shops. They charge a high price but you get your money's worth.

JACHNE-BRAINE: You'll see what you get when you're forced to sell it. A fat lot, you'll get.

TILLE: Leave off. You'll see. We'll be rich, the wealthiest people in the town. We'll move into a great stone house, I with my tall handsome engineer...

CHONE: Pah.

JACHNE-BRAINE: She's crazy.

TILLE: If you can imagine something in one of two ways why choose the worse way? I'd much rather think of the good way. I've...

JUDKE: *(Laughs.)* We'll be rich, heee, heee, heee.

A carriage is heard stopping.

CHONE: *(Jumps up.)* Calamity. Someone has come.

TILLE: *(Rushes to him.)* Lie down quickly. Why do you stand there? *(Pushes him.)* Quick, quick. *(Takes his jacket off.)* Lie down. *(Pulls his boots off and covers him.)* Close your eyes!

CHONE: May you close your eyes for ever.

JUDKE: *(Goes to the bench.)* We'll grow rich, we'll grow rich.

A woman and a man enter.

BOTH: Good morning to you.

REB ITSCHE: Good luck to all.

RIFKELE: Much luck.

REB ITSCHE: Reb Chone is lying down. Good morning Reb Chone. Why are you lying down?

CHONE: *(Moans.)* Good morning.

RIFKELE: Good morning Reb Chone and good luck.

JACHNE-BRAINE: Luck? Why do you wish us luck?

REB ITSCHE: The best wishes one can think of are your due. Whom is one to congratulate if not you? Some poor devil perhaps on the birth of his tenth child?

RIFKELE: May all Jews deserve such congratulations. If God were to favour me with a fine treasure I'd give a great feast.

TILLE: And you have to fall ill.

JACHNE-BRAINE groans and looks at the ceiling. CHONE gives her an irritated look.

REB ITSCHE: *(Sits near CHONE.)* Taking to your sick bed hardly goes with finding a treasure.

RIFKELE: *(Sits too.)* It must be the fasting and the excitement of yesterday.

TILLE: Of course. What else?

RIFKELE: That's the way it goes. A poor devil gets hold of some money and he has to fall ill.

REB ITSCHE: Nonsense. Ill? It'll pass. What's wrong, Reb Chone?

CHONE: Here...

REB ITSCHE: A touch of flu? You should take quinine.

RIFKELE: A great deal of tea and raspberry syrup, wrap up well and sweat.

REB ITSCHE: It's the excitement.

RIFKELE: Exactly what I said. Best to call the doctor.

TILLE: He must have rest.

REB ITSCHE: Of course, he needs rest. I can see you don't need any advice from me. Do you know why I've come, Reb Chone? You know we represent the Society for Providing Poor Maidens with a Dowry.

CHONE: *(Nods and groans.)* Yes, yes.

REB ITSCHE: Then I needn't explain any further. I will only say that as soon as it became known how God has blessed you... *(JACHNE-BRAINE groans and sits on the bed. Reb Itsche turns to her.)* Blessed you without a doubt. You're anxious because he's not well. It will pass. Can happen to any man, whether he's found treasure or not. *(To CHONE.)* As I was saying. As soon as the facts were known, we said to ourselves straight off that our society was the first that should have a share of this gift of God. And why? In the first place, because providing poor maidens with a dowry is the first and most noble duty for us Jews – for it complies with fulfilment of the most important of the 613 commandments, namely, Go forth and multiply, and in the second place, our society has always had its eye on you. And if you ask me what I mean by that, I'll tell you – you mustn't be offended...

JACHNE-BRAINE groans.

RIFKELE: Poverty is no disgrace. People of very fine descent, of the very highest lineage, have turned to us for help.

TILLE: They're talking about me.

REB ITSCHE: And so we thought, our gravedigger has a daughter – may she be a blessing to him — who must be married off and he is unfortunately very poor – not of today be it spoken – and so we agreed that if God sends him the right man for his daughter and he turns to us then he should find an open hand.

TILLE: You see, father, I didn't need to worry.

REB ITSCHE: So now that God has helped you and you can give your daughter all the thousands – now you should repay our goodwill toward you with interest. Here is our book, Reb Chone, and if you can, write down such a sum as your heart commands, and, naturally, the more the better, and as a reward God will send you complete recovery from your sickness.

He places the book, open, with a pencil on the table in front of CHONE.

CHONE: *(Groans.)* Tille, I feel sick.

JACHNE-BRAINE: *(Drags herself from the bed to the sofa.)* He really feels sick. He'll really be ill.

TILLE: *(Busies herself with CHONE.)* He must get some sleep. He didn't shut an eye all night.

RIFKELE: It's the excitement. Always is. I know a case where a man was driven mad by a surprise like that. He was poor and suddenly received news of a great inheritance. He went crazy on the spot.

JACHNE-BRAINE: God preserve us and all Jews from the like.

RIFKELE: I was only trying…

TILLE: Best thing for him now is rest. He shouldn't see anyone.

RIFKELE: How were we to know he'd fall ill all of a sudden? Especially as he was in the synagogue last night.

REB ITSCHE: *(Rises.)* There's nothing to be done. I suppose we must come back another time. Never mind, Reb Chone, you won't run away, I know.

RIFKELE: *(Also rises. To TILLE.)* You're here. You can do the giving.

TILLE: Do you think we can worry about anything like that at this moment? Let my father get well first.

RIFKELE: Exactly. May he have the gift of recovery without delay.

Noise off.

TILLE: I think I can hear a cab. Maybe it's the doctor.

CHONE groans loudly. JACHNE-BRAINE wrings her hands and drags herself back to the bed.

RIFKELE: Is it that bad? Did you really send for the doctor?

Another man and a woman enter and are surprised to find the first two there. Somewhat uncertainly, they say 'Good day'. *There is a mutual exchange of greetings:* 'Oh, Reb Itsche', 'Rifkele', 'Reb Chaim', 'Manke'.

REB ITSCHE: Ah, the Society for the Care of the Sick has come as well.

CHONE grasps his head.

REB CHAIM: Look. He's lying down.

RIFKELE: It's the excitement. They've called the doctor.

MANKE: Is he as ill as that?

REB CHAIM: To get ill now is stupid of you, Reb Chone.

REB ITSCHE: That's what I said.

They seat themselves at the table.

REB CHAIM: When a man has money he has no right to be ill.

JACHNE-BRAINE: *(Moans.)* When a man has money...

REB CHAIM: You mean, little mother, illness doesn't have to ask who it visits. I tell you your old man has got off very lightly and so have you all. I read in the paper not long ago that in some place – I think it was Krementshug, or in...no, it was Krementshug – well, that a man received a telegram telling him he'd won 50,000 roubles and when he finished reading it he crashed to the floor and died of a stroke.

RIFKELE: I know of a case...

TILLE: Not a very pleasant subject right now.

REB CHAIM: God preserve us, God preserve all Jews, from such misfortunes. I merely meant to say, you should thank God that your surprise didn't bring worse upon your heads. He's indisposed. But that will pass. Won't it, Reb Chone. Come on, get up. Let's have a brandy and here is our book. Take it and pledge yourself to our Society for the Care of the Sick...

REB ITSCHE: As between the Society for Providing Poor Maidens with a Dowry and the Society for the Care of the Sick, the maidens ought to come first.

REB CHAIM: No. The sick should come first. And we have an old account with Reb Chone so to speak. We are slightly related.

REB ITSCHE: Because you provide his work, I suppose?

RIFKELE: Never mind that. Reb Chone will pledge himself to us first. If for no other reason than we were here first.

MANKE: Go ahead. Let him pledge to you first and then to us for even more.

REB ITSCHE: What do you mean? Is Reb Chone going to make a difference by giving more here and less there?

RIFKELE: He'll give more to each. There'll be enough for all, won't there, Reb Chone?

CHONE: My head is splitting. My head is splitting.

JACHNE-BRAINE: It really is enough to make your head split.

TILLE: You must have a good sleep, father. Why isn't the doctor here yet?

RIFKELE: It's true. We must let Reb Chone have a good rest.

REB CHAIM: The Talmud says if you visit a sick man you take from him one sixtieth of his sickness, and so we are taking four sixtieths and if the little mother will be so kind as to give us something to drink I will take thirteen sixtieths myself all at once. *(To CHONE.)* Why do you lie there and droop your head? You don't know what to do with all the money? Rest assured, you'll know once you're better.

Voices are heard outside the room. Two men enter, calling out: 'Make way, make way'. 'The pious brothers are here', 'The Fraternal Burial Society has come', 'Much happiness to you', 'Where is the brandy?'

RIFKELE: Sh-sh. Reb Chone isn't well.

REB JOSEPH: What? Isn't he? *(Rushes up to CHONE.)* What's wrong? Caught the debtor's fever?

REB FAIVISH: Get up, have a drink.

REB JOSEPH: Drag him from the sofa. How lazy can you get!

TILLE: Have pity and leave him alone. Can't you see how he looks?

RIFKELE: It was the excitement. They've called the doctor.

REB JOSEPH: Nonsense. A doctor for Chone! Isn't he one of the brotherhood? And for us brandy is the best doctor. We don't need any quacks, do we Chone? Eh? Why are you lying there like an old woman rattling your teeth?

CHONE: My head. My head.

REB JOSEPH: If a man has a headache, it is written in the Talmud, let him study, and studying means drink. Get up and stop this nonsense.

REB CHAIM: That's right. That's right. Go for him.

REB FAIVISH: It's an insult to our society. To be lying down when our gravedigger should be offering us a drink.

REB JOSEPH: Bring on the drinks. You should have invited us yesterday, right after evening prayers.

SEVERAL: Out with the drinks. The drinks. He can lie there and we'll do the drinking. We'll drink twice over – once for him and once for ourselves.

They rush up to CHONE and are about to drag him from the sofa. CHONE moans, closes his eyes and puts his hand over his pocket.

REB JOSEPH: Look at our very sick brother holding his hand over his pocket. You can't pull his hand away.

CHONE: *(Groans.)* Tille. Tille.

REB JOSEPH: *(Taking money out of CHONE's pocket.)* Here we are. We have money. *(He shows several bank notes and a few coins.)* The beautiful sovereigns, the golden treasure coins. And banknotes.

TILLE: *(Snatches the money from behind.)* What do you mean taking the money? Putting you hand in another man's pocket? Where do you think you are? The pub? No pity for a sick comrade. You're all drunk.

JACHNE-BRAINE: *(Scarcely able to speak.)* To put your hand ...

CHONE groans.

REB JOSEPH: What? Eh? We?

A cab is heard.

RIFKELE: The doctor.

Silence. The crowd moves away from CHONE and whispers. The PRESIDENT of the Congregation enters. There are shouts of: 'The President, the President.'

PRESIDENT: We have an assembly already. And he's lying down.

JACHNE-BRAINE bursts into tears. JUDKE hisses.

REB FAIVISH: He's lying down sick on account of the excitement.

RIFKELE: They've called the doctor.

PRESIDENT: *(Sits next to CHONE.)* What's wrong with you?

71

CHONE: *(Groans.)* Oh the good God above.

TILLE: You saw for yourself how ill he was last night and he didn't get any sleep. He needs a good rest but it's swarming with people.

> *Those present make as if to go but don't. A cab pulls up. A voice says:* 'The doctor.'

> *All turn to the door. SOSKIN enters with a lawyer.*

SOSKIN: A big enough crowd. Might help our cause. *(To the PRESIDENT.)* You're here too. *(Points to CHONE.)* And he is lying down.

JUDKE: *(Hisses.)* He, he, he.

PRESIDENT: On account of the excitement, he is somewhat – hmm. Best if we go. We must let him rest completely and become himself again.

SOSKIN: I have brought my lawyer, Reb Chone. If he could explain everything to you, you will see that I am right.

PRESIDENT: Let him be, let him be. What is there between you anyhow?

SOSKIN: The treasure was found on my land...

LAWYER: On the basis of...

PRESIDENT: *(Interrupting.)* So that's it. Very well, but leave him alone for now. You get better, Reb Chone. Lie down as you are and have a good rest. You don't have to hurry to get up. You won't be digging any more graves, of course. By the way, when do you plan to move out?

JACHNE-BRAINE: God help us.

CHONE: *(Almost voiceless.)* Why move?

PRESIDENT: You won't want to go on digging graves. We've already chosen another to take your place.

CHONE: *(Sits up.)* Another? *(More vigorously.)* God help me, I'll be left without bread.

Murmuring among those present.

JACHNE-BRAINE: *(Weeping.)* I'm struck down.

PRESIDENT: What do you mean? Left without bread.

REB JOSEPH: It's the fever talking.

REB FAIVISH: He's clean forgotten the treasure.

CHONE: Treasure? Is there treasure? I have none. We'll starve.

JACHNE-BRAINE: God above. What visitation is this?

SEVERAL: How? What? No treasure? Good trick.

PRESIDENT: Quiet. Nonsense, Reb Chone. You can't wriggle out of it with such talk.

SOSKIN: Subterfuge. You have the treasure safe enough.

CHONE: Trick, subterfuge. Yesterday my son buried his dog and found a few coins. I don't even know how many because this daughter of mine grabbed them and ran away, spent everything and spread the rumour that we had found treasure. It pleased her to play the part of a millionaire's daughter.

PRESDIENT: Is that so? Why didn't you tell that story yesterday?

REB ITSCHE: All this comedy is for our benefit?

REB CHAIM: It's all a lie. You have the treasure.

SOSKIN: Be still. Tell me where he buried the dog.

CHONE: How do I know? *(Laughter.)* Do I know where he found it? Do I even know how much he found? Here he is. Let him tell you himself.

JUDKE: *(Mutters.)* In the cemetery,

SOSKIN: Whereabouts? New field or old field?

JUDKE: Don't remember. *(Violent laughter.)*

CHONE: It's no laughing matter. He really can't remember. He's forgotten.

PRESIDENT: Do you expect us not to laugh? What does that mean – he's forgotten?

CHONE: As I live and breathe, he has forgotten.

JACHNE-BRAINE: Clean forgotten. It often happens to him. Especially after one of his attacks. He'll be doing something one minute and next thing he'll go and forget it straight away. Then he can't remember no matter what.

PRESIDENT: Why didn't you tell us this yesterday?

CHONE: Because...because...

VOICES: Ha. Spit it out. Why?

TILLE: *(Who has been staring motionless at the crowd.)* Because it pleased me to play the part of a rich woman in order to get a husband. Does that satisfy you?

VOICES: What. Come on now.

PRESIDENT: Nonsense. *(To CHONE.)* Well, then? Because...?

CHONE: Because we wanted to gain time to find where he buried the dog. Maybe treasure really is buried there.

PRESDIENT: And how did you intend to set about finding it?

TILLE: Seek and ye shall find.

VOICES: Excuses. They're covering up.

CHONE: He put up a board to the dog: Schutschke, rest in peace.

Storm of laughter.

SOSKIN: It's a put-up job. Not a word of truth in it. Yesterday it was the girl who found it, today the boy. They have the treasure.

TILLE: And you heard my father say in the synagogue he found it. Don't believe us if you don't want to. Believe we have the treasure, say I found it, and that we don't want to give it up.

CHONE: *(Jumps up and beats on the table.)* BE SILENT. BE SILENT.

REB JOSEPH: Look at him.

REB FAIVISH: He's quite well.

CHONE: That was her notion. She made me lie there.

VOICES: I said it was a trick. This is a farce.

CHONE: She did it to gain time. If she hadn't...

PRESIDENT: Then we have nothing more to say to each other. We understand the whole affair. But I'll tell you this much, Chone. If your son should remember where he buried his dog or you should discover the place yourself, you are not to believe that the money is yours and belongs to you. The cemetery belongs to the Congregation and so does the treasure.

TILLE: Justice, of course.

SOSKIN talks eagerly to the PRESIDENT, who seems not to be listening. REB FAIVISH slips out, followed by REB CHAIM, who has assumed a serious expression and lowered his head.

REB ITSCHE: *(Looking out of the window.)* It seems to have stopped raining. I have no time at all. I'm late. Good day.

He hurries out. RIFKELE also looks out of the window, says, 'Yes,' and follows REB ITSCHE out.

PRESIDENT: *(Loudly, as if addressing those leaving.)* Whoever finds the treasure will have to share it with the Congregation and the Congregation will decide how much.

MANKE clears her throat and exits.

SOSKIN: *(Loudly.)* Excuse me. That is to say, unless the treasure is found in the new field. I may have sold the...

LAWYER: On the basis of paragraph...

PRESIDENT: We'll discuss that later. Let us not sell the skin before the bear is killed.

SOSKIN: I simply meant to sound a warning. Come, Mr Merkin. Good day.

They leave.

REB JOSEPH: Well, I'll be going too.

He goes.

TILLE: See how the scavengers have spread out over the graves.

PRESIDENT: I think you have heard and understood me, and I mean all of you.

CHONE: Certainly. Do you really believe that if I had found treasure I would not have shared it with the Congregation?

PRESIDENT: So much the better. Since you're not ill, you can move out today.

CHONE: Why?

JACHNE-BRAINE: What's that? Move out?

PRESIDENT: Did I not tell you we have made another appointment.

CHONE: Why? You want to take the treasure and my job?

JACHNE-BRAINE wails.

PRESIDENT: No one is robbing you of your treasure. You have not found it. What your daughter has bought you may keep in peace, along with the bit of money you have. No one demands a share of that. Keep that for yourself...

CHONE: We'll starve to death.

PRESIDENT: There's no agreement that you should remain gravedigger for ever.

JACHNE-BRAINE: For fourteen years he's been gravedigger and now in our old age we are to go without bread. We are to go begging.

PRESIDENT: There's nothing to be done.

He turns to go.

CHONE: *(Beats his fist angrily on the table.)* I shan't move from this spot, whatever happens.

PRESIDENT: If you're going to talk like that, you'll be moved out by force.

CHONE: I won't move even if it's the death of me.

PRESIDENT: Very well, very well.

He hurries out.

JACHNE-BRAINE: *(Runs after him, weeping.)* How can your heart let you agree to such an action? Surely you must let us find a place to live first.

CHONE: You'll not go looking for anywhere. I won't permit myself to be thrown out... There's still the Rabbi, there's still such a thing as a discussion, there's still such a thing as a court... Fourteen years...ah, ah. *(To TILLE.)* You see now, don't you, what you have brought down upon us? Oh I'll... Where's my stick? I'll strangle you. I'll beat you to death.

JUDKE: *(Jumps up.)* No beat her. I'll remember. You see.

TILLE: Go on. Hit me. Beat me. Take a stick or a knife. I could help you look for the treasure after that. You'd better calm down. You've no reason to rant. You're rich even now, and if you need more, there'll be more. Let me take care of that...

JACHNE-BRAINE: *(Returning from the door.)* Oh God, the whole family's coming. Leah and Freide and Gelie and Bendet and...

CHONE: *(As though suddenly awakened, grasps his head.)* Lock the door. Lock the door.

End of Act One.

ACT TWO

The cemetery. Late evening the same day. The rain has stopped but the sky is clouded. A few stars shine through. To the left, two sides of CHONE's house are visible; the front wall shows a door, the side wall two windows. Behind the house is the chamber of rest, and between the chamber and the house is a great gate for wagons. A main path runs from the house, intersected by side paths. Rows of trees can be seen to the right and left of the main path along with wooden huts, expensive gravestones, fenced family plots, plain stones and tablets of wood. A tree in front of the house has CHONE's possessions around it. The cupboard lies on its side against a window with bedding and clothes on it; a bed stands on end against the tree; the sofa stands against the corner of the house, its head against the cupboard and with more bedding and clothes on it. The table stands in front of it sporting a lantern; next to it is the bench; chairs are scattered about. People swarm across the cemetery. Lights wander about. Figures with lanterns come and go through the gate, some in and out of the chamber. JACHNE-BRAINE lies on the sofa. Now and then she groans. JUDKE sits on the bench, making faces from time to time and laughing. A pregnant woman SARAH and her husband AARON approach, lanterns in hand.

SARAH: Oh my back. All that bending.

AARON: What d'you expect? We'll sit for a moment.

They sit on the chairs.

SARAH: What a shame. Today of all days it rains so we can't sit on the grass.

AARON: Would you rather go into the chamber? It's very damp out here.

SARAH: What d'you take me for? I'd die of fright. Every limb is already trembling from prowling round these graves in the dark. At least this is in the open among other people.

JACHNE-BRAINE sighs. The woman jumps up.

Oh my God.

AARON: Don't fret. It's only the gravedigger's wife.

SARAH: *(Sits again.)* I felt all my blood was draining out of me. I thought it was one of the dead.

JACHNE-BRAINE: One of the dead. If only. I am worse than dead. The dead have rest at least. And I haven't even that.

SARAH: I shouldn't have come here at all. The bending's not so bad but the fright. It'll be a miracle if I don't go into labour before my time.

JACHNE-BRAINE: Oh God above, even pregnant women search for the treasure.

SARAH: I assure you if I find it I have a very good use for it.

AARON: Are you rested now? We didn't come here to sit around being idle.

SARAH: Oh, come on then. Let's go.

The man rises. The woman gets up with difficulty, leaning against him. JUDKE laughs. The woman utters a cry, swings round, grasps the man by both hands to steady herself and looks round with wild eyes.

AARON: *(Also looks round. Sees JUDKE and spits.)* That's their son – the loony.

They disappear among the graves, the woman sighing.

JACHNE-BRAINE: *(Looking after them.)* Oh. Big with child. Her time almost come. She'll kill that baby… And you, will you stop laughing? What is there for you to laugh at suddenly, I'd like to know?

JUDKE laughs then falls silent. Voices can be heard among the shadows. CHONE comes through the gate holding something. Not very steady on his legs, he goes to JACHNE-BRAINE and bends over her.

CHONE: Here's something warm for you.

JACHNE-BRAINE: *(Starts.)* Oh, you've scalded me.

79

CHONE: Serves you right. There. Take it.

JACHNE-BRAINE: Can't you see what you're doing? *(Takes the glass of tea.)* Half spilt. You smell of drink. I lie out in the rain and you go and get drunk.

CHONE: *(Sits on the cupboard.)* You better quarrel with that delightful daughter of yours, not with me.

JACHNE-BRAINE: Drunk.

CHONE: I say quarrel with your daughter not me.

JACHNE-BRAINE: May death himself soon have a quarrel with you both.

CHONE: Go, find her. Talk to her. She's looking for treasure. First she stirs up the whole town and now she runs like a poisoned rat from one end of the cemetery to the other and hunts, hunts for the little board... Schutschke, rest in peace...ha, ha, ha. Why didn't I break every bone in her body yesterday? Then we would've known nothing of this misfortune. I shouldn't have let her go yesterday morning. I should have taken all the money, throttled her and broken all the bones in her body.

JACHNE-BRAINE: Why didn't you? Why?

CHONE: I should have twisted her neck – and yours too.

JACHNE-BRAINE: Why mine, you old drunk. Didn't I say at once, take the money from her.

CHONE: I'll tell you why. To be rid of you.

JACHNE-BRAINE: Oh, that I may be rid of you in double quick time. You want to destroy us. Why didn't you let me look for another place?

CHONE: You'd better ask your daughter, the millionaire lady. She will build you a house made of the finest stone. And now be still. Let me sleep. *(To JUDKE.)* And you, stop your laughing. Why do you neigh like a... *(Kicks out at him.)* Shut up. Let me sleep.

JACHNE-BRAINE: He's drunk his fill and now he lies down. What is to happen to us?

> *CHONE turns his back. Various figures carrying lanterns appear and sit down – on the chairs, on the window sill – then jump up and disappear again. Two townspeople, JACOB and YEKEL, enter with MOREVSKAYA a teacher, engrossed in conversation. They head for the bench.*

MOREVSKAYA: You're not listening. My plan is the following. We mustn't look round the headstones at all...

JACOB: This bench is still wet.

YEKEL: We can lean against it. My legs are giving way...

MOREVSKAYA: Will you listen or not? We mustn't search among the gravestones. It's perfectly clear the one they call the mad kid buried his dog either behind the fence or under a tree. Therefore I am firmly of the opinion that...

JACOB: Why is that perfectly clear?

MOREVSKAYA: Why? Very simple. He's not totally crazy and has enough brains left to...

YEKEL: 'Rest in Peace' – that shows sense I suppose.

JACOB: You can't get to the bottom of a madman's mind. It may just have struck him to bury his dog next to his grandmother's grave. *(Eagerly.)* D'you know? That's rather a good idea. I really wouldn't mind knowing where his grandmamma is buried.

MOREVSKAYA: And I tell you, you had better follow me and look under the trees and along by the fence.

JACOB: People have looked all over. Under the trees, beside the fence, behind the fence.

YEKEL: You know the whole town's here?

JACOB: And not just this town. I'll bet there's people from the next towns as well.

Suddenly a woman's hysterical cries are heard. MOREVSKAYA, JACOB and YEKEL get up to investigate. A young woman, crying still, is led in, followed by several people.

JACOB: *(To one of the newcomers.)* What's up?

NEWCOMER: Shock. One of the dead. She thought she saw one of the dead standing right behind her.

ALL: Take her into the chamber.

VOICES: No, she'll die of fright in there. Take her home. Get her to the pub.

The woman is led out through the gate. Her cries are lost in the distance. Several remain sitting, then jump up and disappear among the graves.

YEKEL: Well. Come on, then. Let's look again.

MOREVSKAYA: You'll see. I'm going under the trees and by the fence.

JACOB: Under the trees or on the trees, I don't care as long as we find it.

They all go.

JACHNE-BRAINE: *(Groans.)* They'll be the ones to have a fit. They'll stay so long they'll die. They'll – oh, God knows… oh, oh, oh.

The sky clears and is full of stars. The moon shines. JUDKE laughs and jumps up.

What's the matter with you? What's your problem? For six solid hours you've not stopped laughing. Have you gone completely mad?

JUDKE: *(Whispers to her, almost choking on his laughter.)* You see what I do. I do remember. Oh, I'll do something. Tille taught me. Told me. Oh, I remember. Watch.

JACHNE-BRAINE: You'll remember, will you? Yes, I can see.

JUDKE: I remember… I'm strong… I'll see… Oh, I'll do.

JACHNE-BRAINE: What will you do? What has she taught you?

JUDKE: *(Laughs.)* Wait and see. You see. Oh... I... Tille... smart.

Heard from off:

VOICE OF LITTLE GIRL: I want to go to sleep. I want to go home. I want to go to sleep. I want to go home.

VOICE OF WOMAN: Come on, come on now. Miserable, bad tempered child. I have a chance here to put an end to my misery, and suddenly she is overcome with tiredness.

Three boys come running on with paper lanterns. Two sit on chairs; the third stretches out on the table.

BOY 1: *(Continuing a story he has been telling.)* ... And when he saw him he pulled off his left boot and threw it at him and cried: 'Stop. You are mine.' And at once the fire disappeared and under the boot was a deep hole in the earth and in that deep hole lay the treasure.

BOY 2: My grandfather told me a different story. There was once a very, very great forest with tall, thick trees. It was so dense you could not find your way among them. And in that forest the sound of singing was to be heard, a sound so beautiful and gentle you would think the loveliest voice in the world were singing there. And so sweet was the song that no one could tear themselves away and everyone desired to see who was singing there. But it was difficult to penetrate the forest. When those were found who could make their way among the trees, a great snake came and killed them. Thus no one could learn who was singing so beautifully.

Now, in the little town there lived a very pious man. To this man it was revealed in a dream that whosoever could win through to the place where the song was being sung would find treasure. In this same dream the pious man was commanded not to undertake the quest himself, nor to send another until the chosen one arrived. Now, in the same town dwelt a poor man who was also compassionate. He came to the pious man one day and wept grievously. 'Great Rabbi,' he cried, 'help me.' 'How am I to help you, my son?' asked the pious man. The poor man made answer: 'I have given my last garment to one who had none at all. I have given my last piece of straw to one who had none to lie on. Now I have nothing left and can help no one.'

When the pious man heard this he knew that the chosen one had come, and he spoke thus: 'Fast for three days and three nights and repeat the psalms three times each day and on the morning of the fourth day set out for the forest and make for the place from whence the singing is heard. Count the stones on your way, which you will find to number 314, for so many are the letters with which the name of the Eternal is written. The last stone of all you are to pick up and take with you. When you have entered the forest and see the snake do not be frightened and run away but say seven times, 'Food has come out of the fire and sweetness from strength'. Hurl the stone at the snake. What will come to pass, you will see for yourself.'

The poor man did as the pious man had bidden him. He fasted for three days and three nights and three times on each day he repeated the psalms. On the morning of the fourth day he ventured toward the forest to the place from whence the singing sounded, counted the stones up to 314, lifted the last stone and entered the wood. He could scarcely force his way through; the branches beat his face and sharp twigs scratched his flesh. But he went farther and farther and ever nearer and nearer to the place from whence the singing came. And when he was quite near to it, the song fell silent. From a cavern, a great serpent leapt at him, its jaws wide open ready to devour him. He remembered the words of the pious man. He was not afraid and did not run away but said seven times 'Food has come out of the fire and sweetness from strength'. He hurled the stone at the snake. The snake crumbled and turned into a great pile of money, a veritable mountain of gold coins.

The BOY is silent. The silence holds.

BOY 3: *(On the table.)* I'm wet through...

BOY 1: *(To BOY 2.)* What happened then?

BOY 2: What else could happen? There's nothing more. The poor man, I suppose, took all the money home and became very rich. My grandfather told me no more.

BOY 3: He probably divided the treasure among the poor.

BOY 1: Do you think so? I don't. Treasure is not a bundle of straw. You don't give it away so easily.

BOY 3: I'll get a beating from my mother. She told me to stay at home and look after my little sister, and she came here herself... She'll half kill me. *(He lifts his legs and turns himself around.)*

JACHNE-BRAINE: Get down from that table. You'll break it.

The BOYS jump up and disappear, laughing, among the trees. The PRESIDENT, SOSKIN and a crowd come from the chamber.

PRESIDENT: I have been telling you there's no use in us quarrelling now. Let us wait and see when the time comes.

SOSKIN: But the law is as I say.

PRESIDENT: May your tongue not hurt from saying it twenty times over. I know the law too. Let that suffice. How late is it?

SOSKIN: Gone eleven.

PRESIDENT: Three times I have sent the town crier to bid people stop searching. They will destroy the entire cemetery and find nothing in the process, especially at night. But it did no good. No one moved from their spot. Still, I don't want to call the police. I'll send the crier again.

They disappear.

JACHNE-BRAINE: *(Calling after them.)* Thrown out after fourteen years to lie in the gutter. It takes the heart of a murderer to act like that. Whoever heard such a thing?

JUDKE: *(Angrily.)* Hay, hay. I'll fix... I'll show. *(Laughs.)*

TOWN CRIER'S VOICE: The Council bids you go home now and come back in the morning.

The voice trails off. Men and woman come and go. A group of townspeople, YANKEV, HERSH, and HINDEL, enters with SARAH, the pregnant woman, and her husband AARON.

YANKEV: *(Rests on the bench.)* If he cries out til' doomsday d'you think anyone will go? Nonsense. Specially now the moon's come up.

HERSH: *(Rests on a chair.)* Look at me. My legs will hardly hold me up. But I'm not going. In fact, as I reflect on resting here, I realise that this very minute if I were seeking I should find. *(Gets up.)* I'm off again.

He goes.

HINDEL: *(Also rests on the bench.)* I'd like to go home and have a good shut-eye but I'm not going unless everyone goes. If all were willing... I'm so sleepy, so sleepy. I had such a hard fast yesterday. *(Yawns.)*

AARON: It's so late. Nearly midnight. The dead will soon be up to say their prayers.

SARAH: Don't talk like that. My heart is ready to jump out of my body I'm so afraid. I look and while I am looking I'm frightened to turn my eyes away. I feel as if one of the dead is standing right next to me.

YANKEV: It's true. It does feel spooky here. But to sit and stare into space is worse. It's better when you're searching. To sit here... sooner or later you're bound to see ghosts.

HINDEL: Who mentioned the dead?

AARON: Anyone who's afraid should go home.

SARAH: Oh stop the talking. I fear I'll soon...

YANKEV: Why are we sitting here? Let's go and look. Shall we all go together?

HINDEL: Good idea. And whoever finds it, keeps it.

They all rise and begin to go.

SARAH: I can't look behind me. There, behind us...

YANKEV: Do shut up.

HINDEL: A woman has to talk. She must. *(To SARAH.)* Don't look back, that's all. We're all afraid. But we must stay quiet. So be – *(She puts her finger to her lips.)* and hunt...

They all disappear. Silence. TILLE in her new clothes with a veil hiding her face comes through the gate, approaches JACHNE-BRAINE and bends over to see if she is asleep.

JACHNE-BRAINE: *(Starts.)* Who's that?

TILLE laughs and lifts her veil.

Oh, you. How you gave me a fright. What kind of veil is that? And what is this play acting for?

TILLE: *(Laughs.)* I went to the station to see my betrothed, the engineer...

JACHNE-BRAINE: What? Oh, that.

TILLE: *(Sits on the sofa.)* He was to come at eleven, so I went to the station to have a peek. I guessed the matchmaker would probably be there to meet him. I put on this veil so he wouldn't recognise me. I wanted to see how tall and handsome my engineer looks, my engineer who I might have bought for 30,000 roubles. But the broker wasn't there. So I don't know whether he cheated me and didn't wire at all or sent a second wire telling my engineer not to come. Or perhaps the broker was afraid to show his face and my tall, handsome engineer worth 30,000 roubles had to drive all by himself to a hotel and found no one there to meet him and is now asking around town only to discover that...

JACHNE-BRAINE: *(Pushes TILLE.)* Out of my sight. She can laugh at it all.

TILLE: Don't push me. Don't you see I'm putting myself in his place. I feel awfully sorry for him. The poor wretch comes here thinking he'll fetch 30,000 roubles and a bride to boot, and now he has to go back home empty handed. I'm convinced he's come and that he's here. Several young men got off the train, and they were all handsome – each one more handsome than the one before. At least, that's what I felt. There are times when all young men seem handsome to me.

JACHNE-BRAINE: What do you say to her!

TILLE: But now I'm very tired and there's nowhere to lie down. The scavengers will never grow tired. Oh Judke, why don't you remember? Don't you remember yet?

JUDKE: I strong... I try. I remember. I'll do it. See... *(Grimaces and laughs.)*

TILLE: But you don't remember. I can't wait for you. I'll have to amuse myself somehow.

JACHNE-BRAINE: Amuse yourself? What? Isn't all this enough for you?

TILLE: *(Gets up, takes the lantern from the table and goes off right.)* Nowhere to sleep. I might as well join the hunt...

She disappears.

JUDKE: I follow. I want to see fun.

Follows TILLE *off.* JACHNE-BRAINE *groans. Silence.* JACOB, YEKEL, *and* MOREVSKAYA *approach the bench.*

JACOB: You might as well look for the day that's just gone by.

YEKEL: Why are we doing this? We look and look...

MOREVSKAYA: And the worst part is you hunt, you ruin your eyesight, you bend your back double, and at every moment you are thinking someone else must have found the treasure already.

YEKEL: What if someone really has?

JACOB: Well, they found it. That's all there is too it.

MOREVSKAYA: Wonderful. And we still go on looking.

JACOB: It's like this. If someone finds it they'll not be able to keep it a secret very easily. Treasure's not like a purse you can pick up and slip in your pocket. First, it has to be dug up and then a plan has to be made for carrying it away. And all the time hundreds of others are swarming round.

YEKEL: Hundreds? Thousands!

MOREVSKAYA: Suppose someone finds it and doesn't begin to dig straight away but leaves a mark and comes back later?

JACOB: Very subtle.

YEKEL: No use. The cemetery will be well watched until the treasure is found.

MOREVSKAYA: I don't believe they'll ever stop looking.

JACOB: I won't for one. What've I got to lose? I wander the streets day in, day out, sniffing around but finding nothing. Here I am looking for something definite and I might find it in the end.

YEKEL: Don't you worry. There's plenty like you. They've shut their shops as if it's a short Friday to get here as quick as possible. I'll bet half the shops will be closed tomorrow because they'll all be here.

MOREVSKAYA: What do you expect? I'm a school teacher and I gave the children a half day holiday. Don't you think teachers could use some treasure too?

YEKEL: I'd put up with as many thousands of roubles as there have been sins committed here today.

MOREVSKAYA: What talk. With the graveyard full of people.

YEKEL: You're being silly. That's my point. I myself have seen men and . . .

MOREVSKAYA: *(Hurrying away.)* Idle chatter.

YEKEL: The teacher's flown.

JACOB: Well, what did you see?

YEKEL: You'd really like to know?

TILLE'S VOICE: *(From the right.)* Here! Here! Here! I've found it! Found! Found!

JACOB: Found. Do you hear? The treasure's found.

They all rush off and others appear and leave in the direction of the voice, shouting 'Found.', 'It's found.'

JACHNE-BRAINE: Chone. Chone. Get up. They've found it. Get up. Look at the drunk. Chone. Chone. *(She rises from the sofa and shakes him.)* Get up. They've found it.

CHONE: *(Half asleep.)* Go and have it out with your daughter, not with me.

JACHNE-BRAINE: Have it out with her, eh? You old drunk. The treasure has been found. Look. Here he lies. As if it were none of his business. Will you get up?

CHONE: I won't move out.

JACHNE-BRAINE: Old drunk. *(Gives him a push. He nearly falls down.)*

TILLE'S VOICE: *(Still in the background but nearer.)* Here! Here! The little board! The little board!

People run, shouting 'There it is. There it is.'

JACHNE-BRAINE: *(Wrings her hands and returns to the sofa.)* Oh, she ought to be punished. Oh, someone should take her and…oh, oh, oh. *(She sits, shaking her head.)*

TILLE: *(Behind the chamber.)* Here! Here! Here! Behind the chamber! Behind the chamber!

People rush there. Voices are heard: 'That can't be true.' 'First one place, then another.' 'Now, of all places.' 'Someone is fooling us.' TILLE, without the lantern, creeps forward, rushes to the sofa and throws herself on it face down laughing.

JACHNE-BRAINE: *(With clenched fists.)* Oh, oh, oh.

VOICE FROM CROWD: Look. Coming here as well.

VOICE FROM CROWD: She's pregnant. The contractions…
or maybe it's a miscarriage.

> *A crowd approaches from behind the chamber. At the front, being led, is SARAH, apparently in labour. Next to her walks her husband AARON. She tries to break free.*

SARAH: I won't let you look for the treasure. It's mine.
I buried it. You mustn't dig it up. God's curse on you all.
I won't allow it. What do you need my treasure for?
The whole world's not big enough for you? Why do you
want to rob me? I won't let you do it. I won't let you.

AARON: Help, good Jews, help. She's gone mad. Save us.
Help.

> *TILLE stops laughing, sits and looks at the crowd.*

JACHNE-BRAINE: Woe upon woe. Why don't you laugh, eh?
Why don't you laugh?

> *SARAH is carried out.*

JACHNE-BRAINE: God above. What do you say to that?

> *TILLE stretches out on the sofa, face upward, hands above her head. JACHNE-BRAINE pushes her.*

Off. Why have you taken my place?

JUDKE: *(Far off to the right.)* I remember! I remember!
I remember!

> *A woman's voice nearby him:* 'That's the gravedigger's son.' *Confused shouts:* 'He's remembered.' 'Judke's remembered.' *TILLE jumps up and runs toward him.*

JACHNE-BRAINE: My hands and feet are shaking.

JUDKE: *(Approaching.)* I remember! I remember!

JACHNE-BRAINE: Chone, get up. Judke has remembered. Get up, Chone. Oh, the drunk. He won't be woken. *(Shouts.)* Chone! Get up! JUDKE HAS REMEMBERED.

CHONE: *(Raises his head.)* What d'you want?

JACHNE-BRAINE: Judke has remembered.

CHONE: *(Rises a little more.)* Eh?

JACHNE-BRAINE: *(Mocking.)* Eh?

TILLE: *(Returns, weary.)* Too late.

JACHNE-BRAINE: What do you say to that? Must he cry it out so everyone can hear?

TILLE: There's nothing to be done.

CHONE: Oh my daughter, my millionaire lady. *(He is about to lie down again.)*

TILLE: Don't lie down. You'll witness something soon that will amuse you.

JACHNE-BRAINE: He's lying down again, the drunk.

JUDKE: *(Accompanied by a great crowd, leaps and cries out.)* I've remembered! I've remembered!

Voices shout: 'Where?' 'Where is it?' 'Tell us where.'

TILLE: He'll tell you when he's good and ready.

JUDKE: *(Making his way to TILLE.)* I remember. Hee, hee. I remember. You see. I fix.

The PRESIDENT of the Congregation and SOSKIN jostle up to JUDKE.

PRESIDENT: Have you remembered where you buried your dog?

JUDKE: Yes. I remember, hee, hee, hee. I remember.

PRESIDENT: Where is it?

SOSKIN: The new field?

JUDKE: I'll tell…but I want… I want…

PRESIDENT: What do you mean?

JUDKE: *(Bursts out.)* Won't say.

PRESIDENT: What kind of nonsense is this?

JUDKE: I tell but you do what I want.

PRESIDENT: *(To TILLE.)* Do you understand what he wants?

TILLE: I suppose he has something in his head. He'll tell you soon enough.

CHONE: *(Sits up and rubs his knee.)* Ah my little daughter.

VOICE 1: Let's hear what he wants.

PRESIDENT: What is it you want?

JUDKE: *(To CHONE.)* I want you to get up and *(To the others.)* you – all, all, all, all – what I do, you do same.

CHONE: *(Laughs, a little drunk still.)* Hay, hay, hay. *(Lights his pipe.)*

PRESIDENT: So that's what you want. I'll beat you to…

VOICE 2: He wants to make fools of us…

VOICE 3: The mad boy making a fool of us. No, he's just crazy.

VOICE 4: He's been put up to this.

CHONE: Hay, hay, hay.

VOICES: Show us where now or we'll tear you apart.

JUDKE: *(In a rage.)* Won't show. Never. Forget it.

   Crowd backs away.

TILLE: Do you think you're his master and can beat him as you please? What's it got to do with you where the treasure is?

CHONE: Listen to my little daughter.

VOICE 2: Why have we been here all this time?

TILLE: You won't get a share for all that.

VOICE 1: All right but we'd just like to know.

JUDKE: I run away. Never tell.

PRESIDENT: That's what comes of tangling with a mad boy.

VOICE 3: Why don't we do as he says? What's the difference? We want to know where the treasure is and how big it is. Let's act a little crazy. Take it as a penance.

JACHNE-BRAINE: It's enough to drive anyone mad. The things he thinks of.

CHONE: Hay, hay. That's right. Hay, hay.

PRESIDENT: It seems we are all going crazy indeed.

VOICE 4: Do as he says. Sh! Keep still. The general wants to review his troops.

JUDKE: I show you. I say…you do same…

CHONE: Fine, fine.

JUDKE marshals the crowd into a line. The PRESIDENT, SOSKIN and other well-dressed people withdraw behind the line.

JUDKE: All. I want all.

CHONE laughs. The crowd looks at those behind, who reluctantly join the line, though a little away from it.

Hee, hee, hee.

Silence.

Same. You do same. Hee, hee, hee.

CROWD: Hee, hee, hee.

JUDKE: Hee, hee, hee.

CROWD: Hee, hee, hee.

JUDKE pulls a face. Crowd imitates him.

JACHNE-BRAINE: Crazy. *(TILLE motions her to be quiet.)*

JUDKE: Hee, hee, hee.

CROWD: Hee, hee, hee.

JUDKE: Thieves.

CROWD: Thieves.

JUDKE: Scavengers.

CROWD: Scavengers.

JUDKE: Money grubbers.

CROWD: Money grubbers.

JACHNE-BRAINE motions to CHONE with her hand and shakes her head. CHONE shakes his hand back as if to say, 'Leave me alone.'

JUDKE: Hee, hee, hee.

CROWD: Hee, hee, hee.

JUDKE: Hypocrites.

CROWD: Hypocrites.

JUDKE: Hee, hee, hee.

CROWD: Hee, hee, hee.

JUDKE: All of us.

CROWD: All of us.

JUDKE: Hee, hee, hee.

CROWD: Hee, hee, hee.

JUDKE pulls another face. The crowd imitates him. A woman burst out weeping.

JACHNE-BRAINE: May God forgive us. They're all going crazy.

JUDKE laughs his most disagreeable laugh. The crowd is silent.

VOICE 1: We have gone mad. What's the use of all this?

VOICE 2: What good will it do even if we know where the treasure is?

VOICE 4: There's someone behind this.

VOICE 3: He's got to show us now.

PRESIDENT: This minute. Now. Go and show us.

TILLE: He's not going to show you yet.

VOICE 4: Another trick.

VOICE 3: First him. Now her.

TILLE: *(To CHONE.)* You want to be gravedigger again, don't you father?

CHONE: *(Opens mouth wide as he suddenly grasps the situation. He gets up, walks slowly to the table, lays down his pipe and says with slow emphasis:)* He – will – not – show.

PRESIDENT: What do you mean? Won't show? I suppose we are all making fools of ourselves here for nothing?

CHONE: What do you think? That you are going to take my job away from me and the treasure too?

PRESIDENT: Take it away? Take it away? You're going to get your share.

CHONE: Of my treasure. My son found it and so it all belongs to us.

PRESIDENT: He found it on land belonging to the whole Congregation.

SOSKIN: In the new field, without a doubt.

CHONE: No use. He won't show you anything. I won't let him. But if you want him to, then I will have to be made gravedigger again.

VOICE 1: As if he'll need the job with his share.

PRESIDENT: So, you want to give up your share in the treasure and instead have your old job back again?

CHONE: Give up my claim? All the treasure's mine. You will get a share.

PRESIDENT: Are you drunk or what?

VOICE 4: He can hardly stand.

CHONE: You needn't worry about my condition. I know what I'm saying.

PRESIDENT: All you'll get is to lose even your own share.

CHONE: Is that what you think? We'll see. Go ahead. Hunt for the treasure. He won't show you where it is.

PRESIDENT: *(To JUDKE.)* Don't listen to your father. He's drunk. Tell me. I am the President of the Congregation.

CHONE: He won't tell you. You may depend on it.

TILLE: What a leader of the community. Teaching the boy not to obey his father.

VOICE 2: Make him gravedigger again and let his son show us the place so the whole thing can come to an end. Why should we stand around here?

VOICE 3: And pretend to be mad into the bargain.

VOICE 4: What do we get out of it if the boy shows us? I'd rather find it myself.

PRESIDENT: That's precisely what you should all have done.

TILLE: And, naturally, you will find it at once now.

VOICE 1: The whole town's been searching and can't find it.

VOICE 2: For a year we may be looking and not find it.

VOICES: Make him gravedigger again. Make him gravedigger again.

SOSKIN: *(To the PRESIDENT.)* What objection do you have? Let him be the gravedigger.

CHONE: For fourteen years I was gravedigger. I worked hard and loyally. No one had a bad word to say of me. The whole town is gathered here. Let anyone who has a bad word to say speak now.

VOICES: He's right. It's true. What do they want of him?

CHONE: Am I to be kicked out after fourteen years? I want to be gravedigger again. I want to be gravedigger as long as I want to be.

VOICES: Yes. Let him be gravedigger again.

PRESIDENT: *(To crowd.)* Who is asking your opinion?

VOICES: That's him all over. Lording it over the town.

SOSKIN: *(To the PRESIDENT.)* Why not? Let him have the job.

PRESIDENT: Suppose the whole thing is a fraud? We make him gravedigger again and then discover his son knows nothing or has not remembered at all.

TILLE: You're just wriggling.

JUDKE: I remember. Sure as I am a Jew. I tell.

CHONE: Judke, be silent.

SOSKIN: Consider. If it is a fraud, you can deprive him of the position again.

TILLE: Exactly. What's there to be afraid of?

VOICE 2: If I were Chone, I wouldn't let them bargain with me, and the Council could whistle for the treasure.

TILLE: But you see we happen to be honest folk.

PRESIDENT: Very well, then. Let him be gravedigger again. *(To JUDKE.)* Now tell us.

CHONE: Oh, oh. He's to tell you now and that's it, eh?

PRESIDENT: What more do you want?

CHONE: In black and white.

PRESIDENT: Doesn't it satisfy you I've said it in front of the whole town? What do you take me for?

SOSKIN: You mustn't blame him. You can see how drunk he is.

CHONE: Drunk or not, I know what I want. And I want to see it in black and white. That Chone is to remain gravedigger as long as he lives or as long as he wants to be. I don't want to be kicked out again the minute it happens to suit someone. I want to give up the job of my own accord or not at all.

VOICE 1: He's not as drunk as you think.

VOICE 2: He's right.

CHONE: Write as follows: If Chone's son Judke shows the right place where he has buried his dog then Chone will be made gravedigger again and will have the position as long as he lives or as long as he himself desires. And if treasure is found in the grave of the dog, or any amount of money at all, one half is to belong to Chone and the other half to the Congregation.

SOSKIN: No, that's ridiculous. You can't sign that. The treasure may be in the new field.

CHONE: If it is, you may go to law.

VOICE 2: What does that man Soskin want? Why does he quarrel about the share? The world isn't big enough for him.

PRESIDENT: The old man's audacity is incredible. Now he actually wants half the treasure.

CHONE: A full half. You may well thank me I'm so kind and willing to hand over the other half.

PRESIDENT: All I can say is – you're a great scoundrel.

CHONE: And all I can say is – you're a bigger one.

PRESIDENT: You say that to my face?

CHONE: I tell you what you tell me. I treat people of refinement with due decorum but I won't let you treat me like a pig.

WELL-DRESSED MAN: *(To the PRESIDENT.)* You won't stand there and dispute with him, will you? You can see that he's inebriated.

CHONE: Doesn't matter. Let me be.

VOICE 2: He does better than some who are sober.

PRESDIENT: Am I to surrender to this fellow? Am I to sign a written agreement with him?

CHONE: As you please.

VOICE 1: What's it to be? What are we standing here for?

PRESIDENT: No one asks you to. Go and hunt instead.

VOICE 2: He imagines we would turn the treasure over to him for less than half.

VOICE 3: He'd be lucky to get half from me.

VOICE 4: It's easy enough for him to say, 'Go and hunt.' Means nothing to him if we neglect our business and wander the cemetery night and day.

WELL-DRESSED MAN: *(To the PRESIDENT.)* If he wants a signature, give him a signature...

PRESIDENT: *(To CHONE.)* You'll remember this.

CHONE: We'll see. *(To crowd.)* Anyone have paper and pencil?

MOREVSKAYA: I have. *(Makes her way through crowd.)*

CHONE: Can you write?

MOREVSKAYA: Why would I be carrying writing material with me? What a question. I happen to teach writing.

CHONE: All the better. *(He clears a space on the table. Lanterns are placed there and a chair drawn up. The teacher sits.)* Wait – how did I put it? *(The teacher writes as CHONE dictates.)* 'If the son of Chone the gravedigger, son of Reb Juda, shows the right place where he has buried her dog then the aforesaid Chone, son of Reb Juda and gravedigger to this Congregation, shall be reinstated as gravedigger of God's

acre of this Congregation and remain in office so long as
he lives or so long as he himself may desire. And if, in
that place where the dog is buried, money or valuables be
found, half shall belong to the aforesaid Chone, son of Reb
Juda and gravedigger, and the other half to our beloved
Congregation.' Have you got that?

MOREVSKAYA: It's written.

CHONE: *(Takes paper, puts on his spectacles, reads it through and
turns to the PRESIDENT.)* Now sign it.

PRESIDENT: This is the first time anything like this has
happened to me.

VOICE 2: The old man's smart. We didn't really know him.

CHONE: If nobody touches me, I touch nobody. But if…
(He takes the paper and reads.) Chaim, son of Reb Mordche
Sackheim, President of the Congregation.

SOSKIN: And I tell you for the final time, you'll have trouble
with me before this is all over.

VOICE 4: There he is again. Poking his nose in.

CHONE: *(Folds paper and puts it in his pocket.)* Go, Judke,
and show them.

JUDKE: Hee, hee, hee.

*He runs off. The crowd applauds and follows, laughing and
shouting.*

TILLE: That was good. Now for the treasure.

She runs off too.

CHONE: *(Begins to run. Stops. Turns to JACHNE-BRAINE.)* Put our
things back in the house. I'll go to the treasure.

He hurries off.

JACHNE-BRAINE: *(Rises from the sofa.)* What a visitation.

She picks up things and carries them into the house.

VOICES: He buried the dog in the grave of the Holy Rabbi. The grave of a saint. The grave of a holy man. The crazy fool.

JACHNE-BRAINE: *(Returning from the house, shaking her head.)* Oh that he may be...

VOICES: He probably wanted his dog to go to heaven. Ah, the little board. There's the dog. How about the money? The treasure?

JACHNE-BRAINE: *(Carrying a heap of bedding.)* Oh my legs. *(She sits.)*

VOICES: That's for burying the dog in the grave of a holy man. That's for burying him at all. That's for all your crazy doings.

JUDKE escapes, carrying the dog.

JUDKE: Leave me alone. Leave me alone.

He rushes out of the gate.

JACHNE-BRAINE: Serves him right.

VOICES: How many coins? Four? What? Four? No more? That's the whole treasure? A splendid treasure. A very fine treasure. Dig deeper. Maybe there's more. And for that they dig up the grave of a holy man.

JACHNE-BRAINE bursts out wailing as if at a funeral.

VOICES: They're digging another corner. No shame. The grave of a holy man. Nothing. Like the day that's just gone. They can look as long as they like. Only four sovereigns.

The crowd begins to melt away.

VOICES: Call that treasure. So much for the famous treasure. Lost a whole night for nothing. And they've dug up the grave of a holy man. How could anyone bear to do such a thing?

A group emerges on its way to the gate.

REB JOSEPH: What people won't do for the sake of money.

MANKE: And whose money? Who would have benefited?

REB JOSEPH: The town.

MANKE: Fat lot the town would have seen with Chaim Sackheim hovering over the treasure.

MOREVSKAYA: Even if the town had got some of the money, what good would it have done?

They leave. Another group emerges.

REB FAIVISH: How did it cross the mind of the crazy boy to bury his dog?

REB ITSCHE: For that alone Chone should lose his job.

RIFKELE: How can he help having a crazy son?

REB CHAIM: If they'd found something in another corner, Chone would have no right to demand a share at all...

They leave. Another group of the well-to-do emerges.

PRESIDENT: *(To SOSKIN.)* Law or no law, you wouldn't have received a kopek.

SOSKIN: And I tell you that...

They leave. Others leaving laugh and chatter.

VOICES: Treasure. There you have your treasure. All that fuss for four sovereigns. The way they let themselves be led by the nose. An able girl, that Tille. A girl in a thousand. She deserves a husband. If she had a dowry, I'd take her on the spot...

CHONE: *(Creeping on towards the weeping JACHNE-BRAINE.)* Treasure, eh? A magnificent treasure. Well, at least the whole business hasn't cost us anything. I've stayed as gravedigger. So what are you howling for? Enough. Come, let's take our things back inside.

He gathers more belongings as he hums.

JACHNE-BRAINE: But if it was so near, and maybe we could have...

CHONE: Go. Don't be so stupid. Everything she must weep about, everything.

TILLE comes on laughing.

JACHNE-BRAINE: She laughs. Oh, that I could drown you in my bitterness. She laughs. You'll not be able to show your face in town again.

TILLE: What? Not show my face? What have I to be ashamed of? Let them be ashamed? I got the better of them all... On the contrary, I shall walk through the town with my head held high... For one day at least I was a millionairess. And... I have some money in the bank as well.

CHONE and JACHNE-BRAINE: What?

TILLE: You heard. It's not a great deal to be sure but enough to catch a man. A very modest catch maybe, but perhaps not so modest after all. I'm such a celebrity in town now and I have the clothes...

CHONE: Jachne-Braine, Jachne-Braine.

JACHNE-BRAINE: Why didn't you tell us this before?

CHONE: I must have a drink to celebrate. Let's go in. *(To TILLE.)* Oh you... The things that you... Well... you deserve to have a good beating.

TILLE: *(Thrusts her face forward.)* Here.

CHONE breaks out into a mighty laugh. They all go into the house. The dim glow of a lighted candle appears in the window of the house. Their faint voices can just be heard. Laughter. Silence. In shrouds and prayer shawls the dead appear singly and in groups. In the moonlight they are seen only in silhouette. They whisper and breathe their words.

DEAD: Swiftly into the synagogue. Hurry. The hour of midnight is long past. Hurry.

They move toward the gate.

I thought we wouldn't come out today at all.

The dead fear the breath of the living.

We fear them more than they do us. There is no peace between life and death.

No peace…no peace…

Life annoyed me greatly today.

Annoyed is not the word. I lived in their life so completely that I shuddered and feared.

Did you shudder with dread or desire? Did you feel a longing for your treasure?

They laugh.

The well-bred and the well-heeled must have had a bad day.

It reeked of money and they had to lie with the worms.

It almost hurled them out of their graves.

SEVERAL: Money…money…money.

They laugh.

But you poor ones didn't have a much better time either. It stank of money and you couldn't even go begging.

More laughter.

It's high time you forgot about life. Quickly. To the synagogue.

A group leave.

I felt quite superior to see how little they feared us.

Don't flatter yourself. We'd have been no better. We were no better.

SEVERAL: Money…money…money.

SEVERAL: That is life…that is life…that is life.

I felt something too. So many women walked over my grave. Young ones, pretty young ones…

Laughter.

Who's talking like this? Uttering such ugly words?

It's the field surgeon who's buried beneath the wall.

HOLY RABBI: *(Passing through, with his prayer shawl hanging loosely over his left shoulder. He has no right arm.)* They dug up my entire grave… They dug up my right arm… How shall I now put on my prayer shawl? How shall I appear before God? *(To a group of the dead.)* Will no one help me put on my shawl?

> *He is helped. Murmurs of compassion greet the discovery of his missing arm.*

SEVERAL: Money…money…money.

RABBI: Now I can appear before God. I will go and ask Him…

> *He leaves.*

DEAD: He will get no answer… He will get no answer.

They who are in life still stand at the same point. Generation after generation dies and all remains as it has been. As it was before time, so it was in my time and so it is today.

SEVERAL: Money…money…money.

And yet it must lead to something.

Surely there must be a goal.

Only God knows that…

But the living must learn what it is.

And that will be their greatest victory.

Man's greatest victory.

SEVERAL: Our…our…our…

SEVERAL: The living…and us?

> *Laughter and sighing.*

Greatest victory…

> *The End.*

COLIN CHAMBERS, a former journalist and theatre critic, was Literary Manager of the Royal Shakespeare Company from 1981 to 1997, and since 2014 has been Emeritus Professor of Drama at Kingston University. He is co-author with Richard Nelson of *Kenneth's First Play* and *Tynan* (both produced by the Royal Shakespeare Company), and he selected and edited for performance *Three Farces* by John Maddison Morton, which were performed at the Orange Tree Theatre, Richmond. As well as editing and contributing to the *Continuum Companion to Twentieth Century Theatre*, he has written extensively on the theatre, including the books *Other Spaces: New Writing and the RSC*; *Playwrights' Progress* (with Michael Prior); *The Story of Unity Theatre*; *Peggy: the Life of Margaret Ramsay, Play Agent* (winner of the inaugural Theatre Book Prize); *Inside the Royal Shakespeare Company*; *Here We Stand: Politics, Performers and Performance – Paul Robeson, Isadora Duncan and Charlie Chaplin*; and *Black and Asian Theatre in Britain: A History*.

www.ingramcontent.com/pod-product-compliance
Ingram Content Group UK Ltd.
Pitfield, Milton Keynes, MK11 3LW, UK
UKHW022130020325

455697UK00009B/121